'7

Beyond
Gay or Straight

ISSUES IN LESBIAN AND GAY LIFE

Beyond Gay or Straight:
Understanding Sexual Orientation

JAN CLAUSEN

MARTIN B. DUBERMAN,
General Editor

CHELSEA HOUSE PUBLISHERS
Philadelphia

CHELSEA HOUSE PUBLISHERS

EDITORIAL DIRECTOR Richard Rennert
COPY CHIEF Robin James
PICTURE EDITOR Judy Hasday
ART DIRECTOR Sara Davis
PRODUCTION MANAGER Pamela Loos

ISSUES IN LESBIAN AND GAY LIFE
SENIOR EDITORS John Ziff, Sean Dolan
SERIES DESIGN Basia Niemczyc
COVER DESIGN Alison Burnside

Staff for BEYOND GAY OR STRAIGHT
ASSOCIATE EDITOR Therese De Angelis
ASSISTANT EDITOR Annie McDonnell
PICTURE RESEARCH Matthew J. Dudley

First Printing
1   3   5   7   9   8   6   4   2

Library of Congress Cataloging-in-Publication Data
Clausen, Jan.
Beyond Gay or Straight/Jan Clausen; Martin Duberman, general
editor.
p. cm.—(Issues in lesbian and gay life)
Includes bibliographical references (p.   ) and index.
ISBN 0-7910-2606-X
      0-7910-2956-5 (pbk.)
1. Homosexuality. 2. Lesbianism. 3. Sexual orientation. 4. Homosexuality— Genetic
aspects. 5. Heterosexuality. I. Duberman, Martin B. II. Title. III. Series.
HQ76.25.C53 1996   95-9398
306.76'6—dc20   CIP
                                                             AC

▣ *Contents* ▣

▣ *Issues in Lesbian and Gay Life* ▣

Other titles in preparation

How Different?

MARTIN DUBERMAN

Just how different *are* gay people from heterosexuals? Different enough to support the common notion that they form a subculture—a shared set of group attitudes, behaviors and institutions that set them distinctively apart from mainstream culture? Of course the notion of the "mainstream" is in itself difficult to define, given the many variations in religion, region, class, race, age and gender that in fact make up what we call "the heartland." And the problems of definition are further confounded when we broaden the discussion—as we should—from the context of the United States to a global one.

The question of the extent of "differentness"—of "queerness"— is subject to much debate, within as well as without the lesbian and gay world, and there are no easy answers for it. On one level, of course, all human beings share commonalities that revolve around basic needs for nurturance, affiliation, support, and love, and those commonalities are so profound that they dwarf the cultural differences that set people apart.

Besides, it often isn't clear precisely what differences are under scrutiny. If we confine the discussion to erotic and affectional preference, then gay people are obviously different because of their primary attraction to members of their own gender. But what more, if anything, follows from that? Gay conservatives tend to believe that nothing follows, that aside from the matter of erotic orientation, gay people are "just folks"—just like everyone else.

But gay radicals tend to dispute that. They insist gay people have had a special history and that it has induced a special way of looking at

7

the world. The radicals further insist that those middle-class gay white men who *deny* that their experience has been unusual enough to differentiate them from the mainstream are suffering from "false consciousness"—that they *are* more different—out of bed, as well as in—than they themselves would like to admit.

If one asked the average person what it is that sets gay men and lesbians apart, the likely answer would be that gay men are "effeminate" and lesbians "butch." Which is another way of saying that they are not "real" men or "real" women—that is, that they do not conform to prescribed cultural norms in regard to gender. It is true historically, that "fairies" and "dykes" *have* been the most visible kind of gay person (perhaps because they were unable to "pass"), and over time they became equated in the popular mind with *all* gay people.

Yet even today, when gay men are often macho-looking bodybuilders and "lipstick" lesbians playfully flaunt their stereotypically feminine wiles, it can still be argued that gay people—whatever behavioral style they may currently adopt—are, irreducibly, gender nonconformists. Beneath many a muscled gay body still lies an atypically gentle, sensitive man; beneath the makeup and the skirts often lies an unusually strong, assertive woman.

This challenge to conventional gender norms—a self-conscious repudiation on the part of lesbian/gay radicals—is not a minor thing. And the challenge is compounded by the different kinds of relationships and families gay people form. A typical gay male or lesbian couple does *not* divide up chores, attitudes, or desire according to standard bi-polar "husband" and "wife" roles. Gay couples are usually two-career households in which an egalitarian sharing of rights and responsibilities remains the ideal, and often even the practice. And more and more gay people (particularly lesbians) are making the decision to have and raise children—children who are not trained to look to daddy for discipline and mommy for emotional support.

All this said, it remains difficult to *specify* the off-center cultural attitudes and variant institutional arrangements of lesbian and gay life. For one thing, the gay world is an extremely diverse one. It is not at all clear how much a black lesbian living in a small southern town has in common with a wealthy gay male advertising executive in New York City—or a transgendered person with either.

Perhaps an analogy is useful here. Literary critics commonly and confidently refer to "the Jewish novel" as a distinctive genre of writing. Yet when challenged to state *precisely* what special properties set such a novel apart from, say, a book by John Updike, the critics usually fall back on vague, catchall distinctions—like characterizing a "Jewish" novel as one imbued with "a kind of serious, kvetschy, doom-ridden humor."

Just so with any effort to compile an exact, comprehensive listing of the ways in which gay and lesbian subcultures (and we must always keep in mind that they are multiple, and sometimes at odds) differ from mainstream patterns. One wag summed up the endless debate this way: "No, there is no such thing as a gay subculture. And yes, it has had an enormous influence on mainstream life." Sometimes, in other words, one can sense the presence of the unfamiliar or offbeat without being able fully to articulate its properties.

Even if we could reach agreement on whether gay male and lesbian culture(s) stand marginally or profoundly apart from the mainstream, we would then have to account for those differences. Do they result from strategies adapted over time to cope with oppression and ghettoization? Or are they centrally derived from some intrinsic, biological subset—a "gay gene," for example, which initially creates an unconventional kind of person who then, banding together with like-minded others, creates a novel set of institutional arrangements?

This interlocking series of books, *Issues in Lesbian and Gay Life*, is designed to explore the actual extent of "differentness" from mainstream values and institutions. It presents detailed discussions on a wide range of gay and lesbian experience and expression—from marriage and parenting, to history and politics, to spirituality and theology. The aim is to provide the reader with enough detailed, accurate information so that he or she can come to their own conclusions as to whether or not lesbian and gay subculture(s) represent, taken in their entirety, a significant departure from mainstream norms.

Whatever one concludes, one should always remember that differentness is not a disability nor a deficiency. It is another way, not a lesser way. Indeed, alternate styles of seeing (and being) can breathe vital new life into traditional forms that may have rigidified over time. Variant perspectives and insights can serve all at once to highlight the narrowness of conventional mores—and present options for broadening and revivifying their boundaries.

Beyond
Gay or Straight

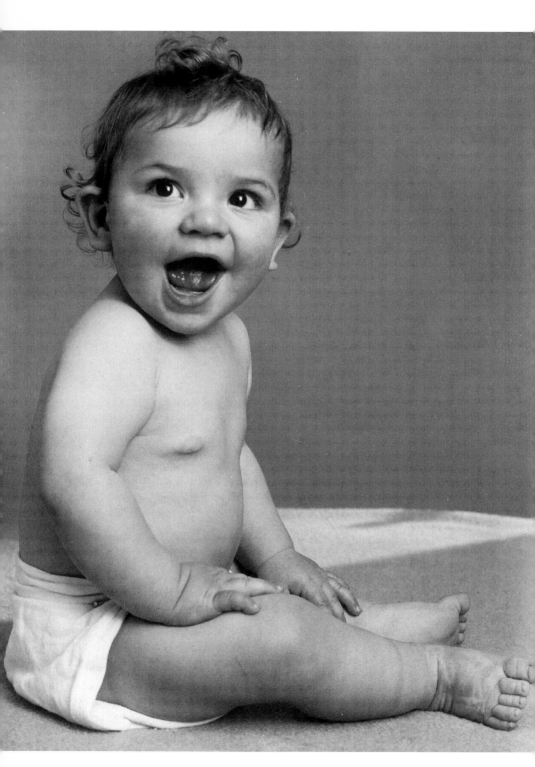

PREFACE

Dear Reader,

OVER THE MONTHS of my work on this book, I have spent a lot of time thinking about you—who you might be and why you would want to read a book about sexual orientation. I imagine you as many different people, all having in common a personal as well as an intellectual interest in my topic. You may have specific questions about your own sexual identity, or that of friends or family. You may be exploring new sexual possibilities, while searching for the right language to express what these experiences say about who you are. Or you may feel perfectly clear about your sexuality, but wonder about its origins, the reasons why you came to have these desires and not others.

The question of what determines the characteristics and qualities that make us who we are has always aroused fierce debate. The argument seems to grow even more emotional when the specific topic becomes what causes, creates, or determines sexual orientation or desire.

You may be curious as to why your sexuality, or that of people close to you, differs from the norm so vigorously promoted by the heterosexual world—that ubiquitous mutual admiration society that gay novelist

Christopher Isherwood sarcastically dubbed "Nearly Everybody." (Or perhaps you wonder why it *conforms* to the norm. As we will see, this is a question that deserves to be asked much more frequently.) You may wonder whether who you are now is likely to shift over time or remain the same for life. You may be wondering: Do I have to choose between gay or lesbian and heterosexual attractions?

Another likely reason for your interest in sexual orientation is that debates over its causes have been so much in the news. You may have heard of the spate of recent scientific studies claiming to find evidence that same-sex orientation in men has a biological basis. Among the most widely publicized are a 1991 study announcing the discovery of significant though minute differences in a particular cell group in the brains of gay and straight men and a 1993 study providing evidence for a genetic influence on male homosexuality. Debates over these claims play a role in hotly contested campaigns for (and, unfortunately, against) gay rights, including ongoing battles over such issues as gays in the military, recognition of domestic partnerships involving same-sex couples, and legislation forbidding discrimination on the basis of sexual orientation.

Far less widely known is an avalanche of studies from a range of scholars including historians, anthropologists, and sociologists. Their work gives us a needed context for the scientific claims and can help us look beyond the questions scientists typically ask, which can usually be boiled down to "What makes people gay?" I call this the causal question because it comes from a model of inquiry developed in the physical sciences, one that assumes that any observed event can be traced back through a relatively simple sequence of effects to an identifiable cause or causes. Scholars in the social sciences and humanities do not necessarily make this assumption.

An obvious problem with asking "What makes people gay?" is that an exclusive focus on this question ignores the need to account for *everyone's* sexuality. Of course, we can also ask, "What makes people straight?" But most experts, even gay thinkers, have neglected this issue or given it less attention.

I believe that theories attempting to explain sexual orientation need to account for the experiences of heterosexuals and bisexuals—as well

as the existence of sexualities not adequately named by existing labels.
(This point actually seemed quite obvious to me until I tried to explain
it to a liberal relative of mine, who shot back a puzzled, "But surely the
need to reproduce our species explains opposite-sex attraction!" The
implications of procreationist—reproduction-oriented—notions of sexuality will be examined in chapter 3.) Because this book is part of a
series on gay and lesbian issues, as well as because of the way in which

*It is often difficult for
people to accept that the
elements that constitute
gender identity and sex-
ual orientation may vary
from culture to culture,
place to place, time period to time period. In
the late 19th and early
20th century in this
country, for example, it
was not uncommon for
very young boys such as
this one to be dressed
and groomed in ways
that today would likely
be regarded as unsuitably
feminine.*

research on sexuality has developed historically, I will spend more time on theories of same-sex love and lust. But I will always be concerned as well with how those theories reflect back on the question "What makes people straight?"

In addition to their neglect of opposite-sex relations, scientists interested in the causal question tend to neglect lesbians in favor of gay males. This follows from the fact that a number of the researchers are themselves gay men who are trying to understand their own identities and desires. It is also predictable given that women's sexuality (whether lesbian or heterosexual) has rarely been the focus of systematic inquiry on its own terms and is usually studied in relationship to men's, using male-oriented models.

This approach is inadequate, to say the least. It means that most of the current research into gay sexuality reflects the perspectives of white male professionals who are seeking causal explanations for the way they and others like them experience the universe of sexual possibilities. Their work depends on a model of desire and identity that may not be shared by most women; by bisexuals; by gay men who are Latino, Asian American, African American, or Native American; by people living outside North America or Europe; or even by different groups of white American gay men. I have tried to avoid this bias, bringing in evidence that can help with thinking through the issues for a broad spectrum of those whom this society defines as sexually different. When the studies themselves are narrow, I attempt to raise questions about their possible implications for groups not named or considered.

I believe that people's sexual experiences—both what their bodies do and what those actions mean to them—vary widely depending on their cultural environment. Generational differences often mean cultural shifts, so I have included the perspectives of young people whenever possible. My informants are students of high school and college age from a variety of backgrounds who have studied writing with me in New York City classrooms. I am grateful to them for their honesty and generosity in sharing their memories and thoughts, and especially for permission to quote from their comments and writing.

If you are going to spend an entire book with me, you deserve some sense of who I am. Just as I believe that a student's cultural environment or a scientist's life experience affects how she or he approaches sexual questions, so I recognize that my background has much to do with the way I have approached the writing of this volume. It matters, for instance, that I am one of those people who never felt a strong sense of having a fixed, unidirectional sexual orientation. (Which does not mean that I doubt the stories of those who say they were clearly one thing or the other from early childhood, just that my own memories are different—and that I believe any useful discussion of orientation has to recognize the existence and validity of both sorts of experiences.)

As a little girl living in a white, middle-class nuclear family in a small northern California town in the 1950s, I had erotic fantasies involving adult women that I can now interpret as "lesbian"; I also assumed that I would grow up to like boys and get married. As an adolescent, I had my first passionate sexual affair with a young man my own age. I can remember being anxious about whether I was playing the appropriate gender role; if the female role is passive, I thought to myself, is it appropriate for me to put my tongue in his mouth if we kiss? Shouldn't it be the other way around?

As I entered my twenties, I became involved with the feminist movement of the early 1970s, and about the same time I began to make love with women. At 25 I fell in love with a woman who would be my lover for the next 12 years. Together we raised a daughter (biologically hers), helped found a lesbian literary magazine, and engaged in a range of political and cultural activism: everything from organizing support for the Nicaraguan revolutionaries known as the Sandinistas to publishing a group of feminist essays on anti-Semitism and racism.

Throughout this time I considered myself a lesbian pure and simple, even though I realized that I had never completely shed my capacity for physical attraction to men. ("It's not their bodies that are such a turnoff, it's their attitude," was one of my lines.) Then, in 1987, I fell in love with a man, and my identity as a woman-loving woman seemed to shatter.

I have written in some detail about that experience in an essay called "My Interesting Condition," which is listed in the Further

"A kiss is just a kiss," the old song claims, but a kiss's significance varies based on any number of elements that make up the context in which the act takes place.

Reading section at the end of this volume. What matters for you to know here is that the transition I underwent has made me profoundly suspicious of the adequacy of any labels, including bisexual, for my own sexuality. I now live with my male companion, which makes me a "practicing heterosexual" in everyday life. Yet in terms of social ties, intellectual interests, and political concerns, I move back and forth between gay and straight worlds.

In my work as a writer and teacher, I continue to be widely perceived as a lesbian (especially by heterosexuals) because I consistently speak out on lesbian and gay issues. I do so not only out of a commitment to justice and a concern for my gay friends and my lesbian daughter but out of the awareness that, no matter my future sexual choices, my chances of living in a world that can understand my books and actions depend directly on the achievement of greater freedom for lesbians and gays. My complicated life makes me vividly aware that "homosexual" and "heterosexual" (though not, I think, "bisexual") are names for cultural as well as sexual categories. For instance, there are lesbian jokes, gay in-group references, and ways of viewing the world that I am comfortable with because of what my community is, not who I am sleeping with.

The issue of my own slippery identity raises the question of the terms I will be using in this work to refer to sexual and political categories. (For further information, consult the Glossary at the end of this book.) To begin with, I use the phrase "sexual orientation" (not "sexual preference," "lifestyle," or "sexual status") to suggest what I believe to be the deep—though not necessarily unchanging—location of particular forms of desire within the structures of the self. "Sexual orientation" is the term preferred by most lesbians, gays, and bisexuals because it contradicts the notion that desire can change at will.

When speaking of modern Western cultures, I will tend to use "homosexual" interchangeably with "gay male" or "lesbian." "Homosexual," however, has broader, less political connotations; it is especially useful for describing instances of same-sex behavior in which equivalents to the categories "lesbian" or "gay" do not or did not exist for the individuals involved. For instance, it makes sense to say that male homosexual behavior was common in ancient Athens or is found to be prevalent among certain Melanesian tribes. To refer to these activities as "gay sex" would only confuse the issue.

I find it personally difficult to accept the term "bisexual," since it suggests a parallel to homosexual and heterosexual orientations, when in fact what I and many others have experienced seems to be a combination of lesbian or gay and straight identities and desires. However, we need a word that points to the fact that for many people sexuality is far less clear-cut than the usual dichotomy of gay or straight allows. For the

Certainly at this time in American society, most people are likely to have far different reactions to this kiss between Sergio Cordova (left) and Jim Quinlan, which took place on the Mall in Washington, D.C., during the March for Lesbian and Gay Rights in April 1993, than they would to the kiss shown in the previous photograph in this chapter.

time being, then, bisexual is the best alternative.

"Heterosexual," like "homosexual," combines a somewhat clinical sound with the advantages of relative political neutrality. When used as an adjective, like "homosexual," it conveniently describes relationships and behaviors not adequately understood by current Euroamerican categories, which assume that the sex of one's erotic partners says something supremely important about who one is in the world. The concept of "heterosexuality" as an *identity* is—like that of "homosexuality"—a strictly modern phenomenon, as chapter 3 will illustrate. "Straight" is

often used as an antonym for "gay," a colloquial term for a modern identity.

Finally, I occasionally find certain informal terms useful because the more neutral, sanitary-sounding language has so often been used to hide our strong feelings about sexuality. Lesbians and gays have sometimes adopted words like "dyke," "faggot," and "queer," attempting to reclaim in a positive way language that has been used against them by the dominant culture. There continue to be fierce debates about this tactic. "Queer" is the most recent term to be widely reclaimed and is sometimes used to include a broad range of sexual identities that have been treated as deviant by mainstream society, such as dominant-submissive practices, irrespective of whether the partners are of same or opposite sexes.

This is a book not of answers but of questions that lead to further questions. Or at any rate, the answers will not be handed to you prepackaged. My plan is to share with you some of the vast and growing body of knowledge about sexual orientation; to lead you through the tangled webs of assertion and counterargument that stem from and contribute to that knowledge; to help place in historical perspective the strong emotions evoked by these debates; to investigate the debates' social context, including the ways in which they have commonly been reported; and, finally, to leave you with tools to help you fashion your own answers.

The fact is that there is no expert consensus on much of anything in this field. For instance, not only are answers to the causal question ("What makes people gay—or straight, or bisexual?") in hot dispute but leading schools of thought differ on whether it even makes sense to pose the question in those terms in the first place. This suggests to me that an open-ended approach is the only honest one. Furthermore, I am convinced that the topic of sexual orientation—like other topics often left to professional opinion, from the budget deficit to genetic engineering—affects all our lives on too significant a level to be entrusted to the "experts."

Accordingly, the first part of this book is concerned with establishing the terms of the current debates and with providing a cross-cultural and historical context within which to view them. Knowledge of the many ways in which societies organize sexual relationships may make us more inclined to wonder about the sexual possibilities available in given situations, and less inclined to look for common sexual types that surface time and again throughout history. We can begin to see that the way in which sexual identity is most often defined in North America and Europe (with heterosexual, lesbian, and gay as the widely recognized though not equally accepted options, and bisexual as an emerging alternative) is by no means universal. We will consider some features of other existing arrangements.

Doing so will not, however, necessarily make us abandon our curiosity about the origins of those desires for the same or the opposite sex that loom so large in our culture. We will therefore want to come back to the causal question, looking at a variety of answers offered by past generations as a necessary context for understanding recent scientific studies. We will then spend a good deal of time figuring out just what the scientists are currently claiming and what criticisms have been made of their claims, both by other scientists and by social thinkers.

At last we will want to return to larger issues surrounding the claims and counterclaims, to ask such questions as: Why does establishing a cause for sexual orientation matter so much to so many? Could doing so help us to live better lives? In the absence of causal explanations, how might we account for who we are? What's the best way to fight for that most basic of freedoms, the one that has been called "our right to love"?

Yours truly,

Jan Clausen

1

What Is All the Shouting About?

WHEN I MENTIONED I was writing a book on the sexual orientation debate, a gay historian responded, "You've taken on a difficult job—it's such an emotional topic!" That was an understatement. Particularly within lesbian, gay, and bisexual communities, passions run high over three fundamental, and fundamentally connected, questions relating to the origins and nature of sexual orientation. Before engaging with the specifics of the debate, it makes sense to take a look at those questions and the emotional charge they carry, which is rooted in the gay and lesbian past.

Vase paintings depicting homosexual relations between males were common in ancient Greece, reflecting societal acceptance of such activity.

1. Is sexual orientation an inborn trait, or does it somehow develop in the unfolding personality?

2. Is it an unchanging characteristic, or one that's liable to shift over time?

25

3. Is it present in all cultures, even those that appear to organize sexuality quite differently from the way we do, or is it simply the way in which certain societies (especially Western, urbanized ones) currently think about personal sexual identity?

The either/or format in which I've phrased these questions is somewhat misleading; as we will see, many people have proposed compromise answers (for instance, the notion that sexual orientation arises out of some interaction between inborn traits and the child's experiences). Nevertheless, for the purposes of beginning our discussion, it is useful to set them out in the simplest terms possible, both as an aid to understanding and because most thinkers tend to come down more or less on one side or the other.

The debate arouses such strong emotions because each of the three questions is resonant with the history of the public emergence of lesbian and gay peoples and their struggles against persecution. Even today, many gay people spend childhood and adolescence aware of a difference they must try to conceal out of fear of rejection, ridicule, or physical abuse. Several decades ago, before the self-creation of large, visible gay communities and movements, this was an even more common experience.

For some who have survived such isolation, the notion that their sexuality was inborn seems like an affirmation of its centrality to their lives and offers an explanation of how their identities could have taken root in such unlikely soil. Others argue that precisely because gay peoples and cultures have been so attacked, we have to be willing to argue for everyone's "right to love" on its own terms, without falling back on some notion of destiny or predisposition, and we have to include the experiences of those who remember becoming gay as well as those who claim to have been born that way."

"Are you saying we *choose* to go through all of this?" the first group demands. "Nobody chooses to be persecuted," the second group replies, "and, no, of course sexuality isn't something you pick out the way you reach into a drawer and decide which pair of jeans to wear, but that doesn't mean it's as simple and predetermined a trait as eye color, either. Let's consider some alternative explanations, including the possibility that behaviors we group together under the headings 'homosexual' or 'heterosexual' may have different sources in different people."

Debaters on both sides are responding to an old theme in homophobic campaigns: the effort to coerce homosexuals into becoming heterosexual, or at least refraining from acting on their desires. Over the years, a variety of cruel and ineffective procedures have been utilized in this effort, including many in recent decades perpetrated in the name of psychotherapy. Lesbians and gay men spent years on the psychoanalytic couch trying to recover from what had supposedly gone wrong in their childhoods to prevent them from attaining the "mature" state of heterosexual desire. Behavioral psychologists devised painful aversion "therapies" that used electric shocks in an effort to break the association between homoerotic stimuli and sexual pleasure. Lesbians and gay men were committed to mental institutions, sometimes by their own relatives. In the 1940s and 1950s, some were forced to undergo frontal lobotomies in the belief that this crude form of brain surgery would cure them of their "unnatural proclivities." Doctors in some countries also administered hormone treatments, some of which functioned as a form of "chemical castration." Such approaches are not entirely a thing of the past; in recent years, Eli Siegel's cult of Aesthetic Realism and various Christian organizations have claimed to be able to change gay people into straight ones.

Thus, the question of whether sexual orientation is fixed also provokes passionate responses. Gays who have experienced little or no variation in the direction of their attractions may be more apt to experience pressure to change, since their orientation presents the clearest challenge to heterosexist beliefs that opposite-sex passion should rule the world. They have reason to be especially wary of any theory that seems to lend support to homophobic demands for change, even when progay theorists make it clear that change is not within the conscious control of individuals. People who have experienced more fluidity in their sexuality have a personal stake in a theory that recognizes change. They may be quicker to argue for "our right to love" on the basis that same-sex attraction is just as legitimate and real when experienced by a 50-year old who is conscious of gay feelings for the first time as it is for a 15-

year-old who is beginning to act on attractions familiar from childhood.

Finally, the third question arouses similarly strong emotions because homophobia and heterosexism have so often functioned by silencing or making invisible anyone who does not fit the heterosexual norm. Homosexuality was called "the love that dare not speak its name," as though gay men and lesbians had chosen to keep quiet. But the fact was that society at large engaged in a great conspiracy not to mention that love—and, some would argue, to make the fantasy image of the homosexual all the more powerful precisely because the existence of real-life

Participants in a gay rights rally at the United Nations headquarters in New York City listen to a speaker. Just as there is nothing in the appearance of the individuals here that would indisputably identify any of them as gay or lesbian—if indeed they are—it is impossible to provide a single definitive answer to the question of whether gays or lesbians are "born" or "made."

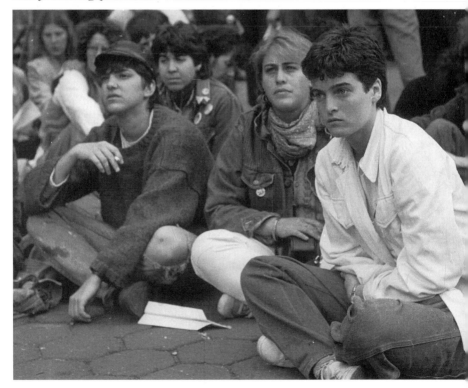

homosexuals in substantial numbers was never openly acknowledged.

With the beginnings of the gay liberation movement at the end of the 1960s, symbolically marked in the United States by the Stonewall Rebellion of 1969, gays and lesbians began to comb the past for hard evidence that this secret-laden silence was a lie. Their own coming-out process and the positive effects of a loud and visible movement had shown them the strength in numbers and in a vigorous public presence. Now they wanted to expand their gains by uncovering their community in history. The resulting investigations have given rise to the current debates, as some researchers retrieved what seemed to them evidence of a hidden and silenced lesbian and gay tradition in many times and places, while others began to suspect that the information they were unearthing about same-sex behavior was being distorted by assumptions that it corresponded to the researchers' own sexual identities.

To suggest that the homosexual as a special type of person may not have existed in, say, ancient Rome, despite ample evidence of Roman men having sex with men, may seem dangerously close to reimposing the old pattern of denial and invisibility. The assertions of theorists that they also want to question the historical existence of something called "heterosexuality" do not help much because the male-female combination seems so universal. Myth, legend, and what passes for history are full of lessons about opposite-sex pairing: Helen of Troy and Paris, Henry VIII and his many wives, Captain John Smith and Pocahontas. Who cares whether those figures thought of themselves in quite the same terms as New York City's former mayor Ed Koch, who felt the need to announce "I'm heterosexual!" to the local media during one of his mayoral campaigns?

As for what most people in the United States understand about non-Western cultures,* much of our information comes from the same heterosexist media sources that tell us about ourselves, while anthropol-

---

My generalization should not obscure the fact that "people in the U.S." are an extremely varied group, including those with strong roots in non-Western cultures. See, in particular, Chapter 2 for a discussion of the Native American berdache tradition.

ogists and other scholars bring their own biases to their studies of unfamiliar sexual arrangements. However you slice it, the dominant message
seems to be that opposites attract.

If history provides lesbians and gays with ample cause to fear any
theory that might seem to allow for an element of choice in establishing orientation or challenge the universality of the category "homosexual," contemporary politics gives many more reasons for anxiety on this
score. In many areas of the United States, right-wing politicians have
discovered they can mobilize constituents (and generate large amounts
of money) by invoking the outrageous notion that gays are threatening
the family and looking for special protections not available to heterosexual citizens. Just as a member of Congress can use code words like
"welfare queen" or "illegal alien" when he wants to play on his audience's racist prejudice against poor African-American women and Latino
immigrants, so in this age of AIDS he need not mention disease to be
assured that his hearers are likely to interpret his attack on so-called sexual permissiveness as a hint that gays are plague carriers.

The use of a distorted image of homosexuality by demagogic politicians in the service of larger agendas provides ammunition for those
who argue that gays need a simple, clear explanation of their sexual
identity and how it got that way. Indeed, some gay activists hope that a
definite answer to the causal question will be a powerful weapon against
homophobia. For instance, the Hetrick-Martin Institute, which has
done outstanding work with lesbian and gay young people, tries to fight
the myth that homosexuals "recruit" children to become gay or lesbian
by citing research they feel supports the notion that "sexual orientation
is determined either before birth or very early in life and no one can
alter another person's sexual orientation." They rely heavily on notions
of biological causation.

Similarly, Gregory J. King of the Human Rights Campaign, an
important gay and lesbian lobbying group, hailed a 1993 research study
that claimed a link between genes and male homosexuality. "We think
this study is very important," King said. "Fundamentally it increases our
understanding of the origins of sexual orientation, and at the same time
we believe it will help increase public support for lesbian and gay

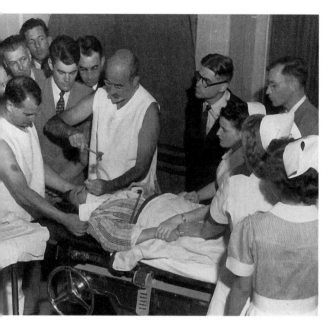

In 1949, a physician drives a surgical instrument of his own devising under a patient's eyelid and into the brain for the expressed goal of severing the nerve connections between the emotions and the imagination, thereby bringing about some desired change in the individual's behavior. Many similarly senseless techniques and theories have been exercised on gay and lesbian patients in an attempt to "cure" them of their homosexuality.

rights." The reporter who quoted King's comments in a *New York Times* article on the research cited the beliefs of "a number of legal experts" that, to the extent that sexual orientation can be shown to be inborn, courts are likely to forbid discrimination against homosexuals. Gay journalist Randy Shilts, author of *And the Band Played On,* one of the most widely read and influential books about the AIDS crisis, told *Newsweek* magazine in February 1992 that proof of a biological basis for sexual orientation would "reduce being gay to something like being left-handed, which is in fact all that it is."

Skeptics respond that simply because a trait is biologically rooted does not mean that it cannot be devalued, and that in fact most attempts at locating genes to explain traits and behaviors zero in on supposedly problematic phenomena. For instance, criminality, manic depression, alcoholism, obesity, and low intelligence—as well as a wide range of diseases—have all recently been explained as the supposed outcome of genetic influences. If homosexuality were found to be based in inheritance, according to this line of reasoning, the homophobes would have a field day with attempts at genetic engineering to "fix" the "problem." Rather than debating causes, we need to work to insure that same-sex desire will be treated as a valid, and valuable, form of human expression regardless of how it is explained.

My sketch of the positions in the debate is, of course, a somewhat oversimplified view of innate or biological theories versus attempts to explain sexual identity as rooted in the social environment, and it bears repeating that individuals do not always line up neatly on either side of the issue. Yet a schematic view provides a useful way to begin to understand the debate commonly described in academic circles as *essentialist* versus *social constructionist.*

In the field of gay and lesbian studies, essentialism refers to the belief that there exist some core defining characteristics of homosexuals that are the same in all times and places. Thus, when considering the same-sex marriage rites from the early centuries of the Christian church researched by John Boswell, or reading about the Indian *hijra* (biological males who are thought of as impotent with women but who attain spiritual power by adopting female dress and mannerisms and in some cases undergoing surgical castration), an essentialist might assume that the observed phenomena correspond in important respects to the phenomena of "gay identity" in modern Euroamerican culture.

Note that an essentialist position does not require a biological explanation for the universal qualities assumed to constitute the "essence" of homosexuality. An essentialist could claim some universal psychological mechanism (for instance, in Freudian theory, the child's effort to resolve the Oedipus complex) as what early Christians in same-sex marriages, East Indian hijras, and American gay rights activists all have in common. She or he could even resurrect the myth propounded in Plato's *Symposium* to explain sexual passion: each human being represents only half of an original dyad, and people are inclined to seek out lovers of the gender with whom they were originally paired.

It is not even necessary that an essentialist thinker specify any particular cause or origin to account for an assumed homosexual essence. An essentialist historical perspective commonly does not take sides on the issue of biological or other causation; it simply assumes that, whatever the cause, same-sex phenomena in different times and places are essentially identical, differing only on the surface as a result of variations in cultural environments and social institutions. Nevertheless, the most influential voices in present-day essentialist thought belong to people who look to biology to explain the origins of sexual orientation.

The essentialist viewpoint is questioned by those thinkers commonly known as social constructionists. Like essentialists, constructionists are a far from homogenous group; many would disagree with one another on a variety of important points. What they have in common is the basic notion that sexuality is best understood as a fluid, changing phenomenon, defined by social contexts that establish not only the meaning but the very texture of what we call experience, including bodily experience. Thus, for them there is no underlying quality or cluster of qualities that characterizes homosexuality in all times and places. Where apparently similar forms of same-sex attraction are discovered in widely diverse settings, social constructionists would advise using extreme caution in understanding the cultural and social contexts of these practices before deciding that what is being observed is really the same phenomenon. Same-sex "marriage" rites in premodern Europe may seem to parallel marriage ceremonies recently devised by gay people who advocate the right of same-sex partners to consecrate and legalize their relationships, but one needs to know much more about how each society conceives of both marriage and sexual pairing (for opposite-sex as well as same-sex couples) before conclusions about the similarity of the two rituals can be drawn.

As anthropologist Carole Vance has usefully pointed out, the most helpful thing about a social constructionist perspective is its role in challenging long-standing assumptions about what is natural and universal. Social constructionists delight in asking new and sometimes audacious questions. A number of them have argued that the word sexuality*itself is in need of examination. They point out that it is used to suggest a supposedly timeless aspect of personal experience, yet draws on an understanding of what is involved in being human that differs substantially from the self-understanding of people in other times and places.

Even 100 or 150 years ago, so the argument goes, people did not

*In 1989, the mayor of New York City, Ed Koch, felt compelled by political con-
siderations to declare his heterosexuality—a declaration about which these demon-
strators against the city's AIDS policies appear to be somewhat skeptical.*

think of themselves as having a sexuality that helped to define the core
of who they were. Of course men and women engaged in genitally
pleasurable acts, which might be socially approved or condemned, but
these were not seen as holding a secret key to identity. It would take a

revolution in both social organization and consciousness—the latter cat-alyzed by scientist-philosophers of sex, the foremost of whom was Sigmund Freud—to forge the specifically modern view of sexuality as being, in the words of historian Robert Padgug, "a separate category of existence (like 'the economy,' or 'the state,' other supposedly indepen-dent spheres of reality), almost identical with the sphere of private life."

One of my favorite illustrations of this viewpoint was provided by a college freshman who had engaged in enthusiastic heterosexual activ-ity throughout her high school career. In a personal essay, she remem-bered how she had suffered as a result of the sexual double standard; she was treated as a slut when she did the things that boys were free to do. She explained the importance her sexuality had for her during those years: "I didn't think of myself as lesbian, heterosexual, or bisexual—I just WAS SEXUAL." Her comment indicates the extent to which she believed that sexual expression, in addition to providing pleasure and emotional satisfaction, somehow marked her as a unique individual. Being sexual was something to be proud of, even though she suffered for it.

The social constructionist point about sexuality is that before the 20th century, for a young woman to have placed something called sex-uality at the center of her sense of identity in this way would not sim-ply have been taboo or considered cause for scandal—it would quite lit-erally have made no sense. The question then becomes: How did this view of certain bodily acts come into being? What promotes it? What holds it in place? How is it changing?

These questions lead in a rather different direction from the causal question as posed by essentialists and biological researchers. The latter group usually wants to know how individuals in any given setting come by their sexual desires and identities; social constructionists are more typically concerned with the range of possible meanings available to those who share a common cultural framework. But this does not mean that social constructionists can ignore the fact that different individuals participate in the same cultural framework in very different ways. So even if we adopt a social constructionist view of sexual identity as being woven from possibilities presented by the sociocultural environment, rather than dictated by biological events occurring before birth, we will continue to ask how identity gets constructed in particular cases.

One might well question the relevance or importance of the entire debate. In the real world that gay men and lesbians inhabit on a day-to-day basis, labels such as essentialist or social constructionist can seem the stuff of academic nitpicking. Often, the antagonists seem to be talking past each other, while varying approaches to understanding human behavior favored by the different disciplines suggest potentially irreconcilable views of the relationship between psychic states and bodily processes. A neuroscientist peers through a microscope at a few brain cells in an effort to discover why some men like to have sex with other men, while an anthropologist spends years with an isolated tribe as he attempts to understand the importance of oral sex (which is routinely performed by all preadolescent boys upon young men of the group) within tribal beliefs about the nature of masculinity. In theory the two researchers might attempt to interpret their results within a single framework; in practice, each is likely to believe, naturally enough, that when it comes to providing convincing explanations, his own field has a corner on the market. Sexual behavior will be seen as primarily shaped by *either* biological or cultural factors.

To further complicate matters, in other instances researchers can use similar methods to examine similar materials, yet arrive at quite different conclusions, as is the case with historical interpretations of sexuality in ancient Greece offered by essentialist John Boswell (who preferred to be called a realist) and social constructionist David Halperin. Basing his claims on his readings of ancient texts, Halperin finds that the ancients viewed lust for one sex as virtually interchangeable with lust for the other. He compares their casual recognition of individuals' preferences for women, men, or both to our notion of tastes for various foods. Boswell agrees that in the classical world the biological sex of one's partner was not regarded as being especially important, but he nevertheless regards those preferences as evidence of something comparable to what we know as sexual orientation.

Time and again, the debate requires confronting questions of interpretation that cannot entirely be resolved by looking at the evidence.

Although innumerable questions about the "causes" of sexual orientation remain unanswered, there is little doubt that intolerance can be taught.

The positions known as essentialism and social constructionism stand for radically different views of what sexuality is, of how to understand human behavior, and even of what constitutes knowledge. Our ultimate objective, therefore, must not be simply to gather information but to clarify and come to terms with the assumptions that underlie the various positions.

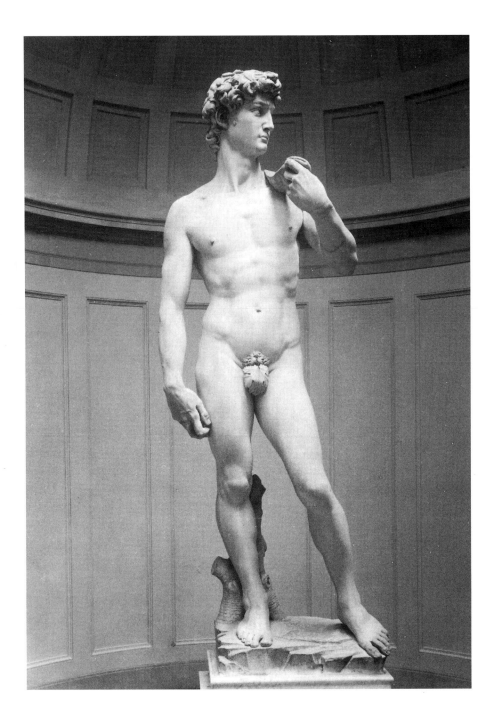

2

Bodies and
Meanings Across
Cultures

*Though few people
would argue that the
beauty of Michelangelo's
David is lessened by the
fact that its creator was
in all likelihood sexually
attracted to men, it has
often seemed that
discussion of the nature
of Michelangelo's sexual-
ity has been excised from
material about his life.*

AS PREVIOUSLY NOTED, CURRENT understanding of same-sex attraction in previous eras grows out of the efforts of lesbian and gay scholars who, inspired by a militant gay liberation movement, set out to fill in the blanks of heterosexist history. Their efforts resembled and in some cases overlapped with feminist attempts to recover "silenced" women's voices, but the task of gay historians seemed even more daunting. For while even the most patriarchal historians could not very well deny that women had been present for the events that they interpreted as the outcome of men's actions, conventional historians typically behaved as though people who experienced same-sex passion had simply not existed—at least not in any significant numbers—before modern times.

Historians thus colluded with those biographers who tiptoed around the homoerotic inclinations of famous subjects such as Michelangelo or Tchaikovsky; with anthropologists who discounted reports of same-sex behavior; and with sex researchers who cloaked their descriptions of "deviant" sexuality in Latin or esoteric technical terminology, lest the lay public be corrupted. Those rare figures like the Greek poet Sappho or the American poet Walt Whitman who declared their same-sex passions openly became icons of the gay movement.

In the 19th century in the United States and Great Britain, very close friendships between young women, even those seeming to contain an erotic overtone or component, were accepted as a normal part of emotional development.

Gay and lesbian researchers went looking in the past for hidden Whitmans and Sapphos. In the United States, the landmark publications that resulted from such inquiry included Jonathan Ned Katz's *Gay American History*, a documentary collection that furnished evidence of homosexual activity as far back as Puritan New England; John Boswell's *Christianity, Social Tolerance, and Homosexuality: Gay People in Western Europe from the Beginning of the Christian Era to the Fourteenth Century;* and Lillian Faderman's *Surpassing the Love of Men,* a history of women's romantic friendships. That such scholarly work threatens heterosexist assumptions is suggested by several newspapers' recent refusal to print a "Doonesbury" cartoon mentioning Boswell's 1994 study of religiously sanctioned same-sex unions in premodern Europe. Homophobia still feeds on the pretense that the whole world was straight until the day before yesterday.

Though the researchers proved the homophobes wrong in this regard, along the way some of them began to be troubled by the consequences of their initial assumptions. They wrestled with what the editor of this series, historian Martin Duberman, has called "the problem of assigning 'gay' or 'lesbian' identities to past figures who lived at a time when those conceptual categories did not exist." He adds that "even today, in many non-Western parts of the world, it is unusual to categorize people on the basis of sexual orientation alone."

This historical riddle is of obvious importance to anyone seeking to understand sexual orientation. Granted that most cultures have not had categories precisely corresponding to our current gay and straight, if even distantly related distinctions can nevertheless be detected within systems that seem on a superficial level to be quite differently organized, then perhaps our categories do in fact reflect some universal (even biological) features. If notions of predictable attractions to same or opposite sex turn out to be completely irrelevant in certain times and places, then it seems clear that culture rather than biology (or any other universal factor) holds the key to the origins of modern sexual identities.

Looking at a variety of cultures can also sharpen awareness of the fundamental strangeness of sexual assumptions prevalent in modern Euroamerican societies—strangeness in the sense that, like all cultural arrangements, they are the outcome of invention, not necessity. Outsiders to a given social system are always in a better position to see this than natives, whose own habits and rituals tend to strike them as natural and eternal.

This "denaturalizing" effect can often be obtained close to home, so I will start with a glance at how several North American groups have organized their sexuality. The investigation will illustrate that the strikingly diverse combination of cultures customarily referred to as "American society" is really no more unified or homogenous in its sexual meaning systems than in other aspects of its composition.

In the dominant American model of sexuality, the two main identity categories—gay and straight—are thought of as mutually exclusive opposites. As such, the terms reinforce one another: notions of heterosexual and homosexual depend on one another in that each one is what the other is not. The third option, bisexual, is less widely recognized and is often thought by homosexuals and heterosexuals alike to refer to people who are confused about their "true" identity, who are either afraid to admit their homosexuality or are really heterosexual but are experimenting. For all three categories, the defining characteristic is the gender of one's desired sexual partners. All other aspects of sexual fantasy and practice are deemed irrelevant.

This model is at odds with much of the history of female same-sex relations in the United States. Historians have demonstrated that white middle-class women in the 19th century, living in a "female world" of extended family networks and strong friendship ties, often developed emotionally intense bonds with other women, bonds that endured over time, had highly romantic overtones, and were described by the participants in language that most people today would consider indicative of sexual passion. Yet neither onlookers nor the women themselves marked off their romantic friendships as sexual involvements. In most cases we cannot be sure to what extent they involved genital or orgasmic sexuality.

In the first decades of the 20th century, women's "special friendships" came under scrutiny. This newly suspicious attitude was in keeping with a greater emphasis on sex in all phases of modern life, a view

Devising an answer to the so-called causal question is complicated by the fact that the terms used to pose the question—gay, straight, heterosexual, homosexual, bisexual—cover an almost infinite variety of behaviors, attitudes, and emotions. Very little agreement exists, however, as to what particular arrangement of these factors comprises the categories themselves.

that distinguished erotic behavior from procreation as important for its own sake. Created in part by women-loving women who found ways to participate in the new ideology of sex as a crucial component of individual identity and personal fulfillment, the figure of "the lesbian" emerged from the shadows. Lesbian novelist Radclyffe Hall, author of the influential *The Well of Loneliness*, drew on the work of sexologist Havelock Ellis, who saw lesbians as a subspecies of "invert," a member of a "third sex." The woman who formed a passionate attachment to another woman would likely be viewed, by both herself and the world at large, as a special kind of person: not a "normal" female whose same-sex attraction was quite compatible with "normal" wifedom and motherhood, but a deviant, at best an oddity and at worst a pervert.

Of course there are significant continuities between the generations. Yet the culturally framed meanings of most romantic friendships underwent a significant shift. This is illustrated by the experiences of Sarah Butler Wister, a Philadelphia wife and mother, and novelist Willa Cather. In 1864, Wister used a male pen name to correspond with her friend Jeannie Field Musgrove, writing, "I shall be entirely alone [this coming week]. I can give you no idea how desperately I shall want you." Twenty-eight years later, Cather wrote to her friend Louise Pound expressing, along with intense romantic feeling, her apprehension that feminine friendships are "unnatural."

By 1892, as Cather's biographer Sharon O'Brien has noted, the word "unnatural" had become a code word for deviance or homosexuality; Cather was aware that her feelings would be disapproved of by the dominant culture. Over a century later, our perspective is probably still closer to the 1892 viewpoint; even if we reject the notion of homosexuality as deviance, our almost inevitable curiosity about what precisely these romantic female pairs did or did not do of a genital sexual nature is the outcome of a distinctly modern outlook, a set of assumptions about the importance of bodily acts in defining the self and assigning it to sexual categories.

The modern trend is toward emphasizing sex. But within that trend there are significant fluctuations. Various lesbian subcultures that have emerged in the decades following the Stonewall Rebellion have differed significantly in the extent to which they have shaped their self-definitions around sexual acts and desires. Lesbian feminists of the 1970s, with roots in the predominantly white and middle-class women's movement, frequently rejected the butch-femme role playing of an earlier generation of lesbians, opting for a model of "woman identification" that sought to expel all male influence from lesbian relationships and create the sexual world anew. Many of these feminists saw lesbianism as the logical response to patriarchy, an embrace of the possibilities of intimacy between women that male culture had denied. Lesbianism involved overcoming an artificial separation between women that had been imposed by masculine "divide and conquer" tactics. This meant not that lesbian feminists were asexual but that same-sex desire might follow an acceptance of "sisterhood" rather than the other way around.

Lesbian musician Alix Dobkin said it all in the sloganlike chorus to a song on her *Lavender Jane Loves Women* album: "Any woman can be a lesbian." The theory received its most eloquent treatment in poet Adrienne Rich's essay "Compulsory Heterosexuality and Lesbian Existence," which appealed to feminists to think in terms of a *lesbian continuum* that would include "all women—from the infant suckling at her mother's breast, to the grown woman experiencing orgasmic sensations while suckling her own child, perhaps recalling her mother's milk smell in her own, to two women, like Virginia Woolf's Chloe and Olivia, who share a laboratory, to the woman dying at ninety, touched and handled by women."

In the early 1980s, feminists furiously debated positions on a range of issues that included sexual fantasies, pornography, and sado-masochism. Within that debate, popularly known as the "Sex Wars," many lesbians contested what they saw as the asexual nature of the lesbian-feminist emphasis on loving women as a political choice. They called for an exploration of the class and race assumptions behind prevalent ideals of lesbian behavior. Often invoking as a positive model the working-class butch-femme tradition, they advocated an emphasis on lesbian desire—that is, explicit sexuality rather than diffuse woman identification—as the defining feature of lesbian identity. The result was a new standard model lesbian much more likely to present herself as an overtly sexual creature, to flirt with or flaunt a butch or femme role, and perhaps to explore sadomasochism or other marginal sexual practices that an earlier generation had been quick to condemn.

It is debatable to what extent these shifting definitions actually affected how women experienced their sexuality. Yet the shifts do demonstrate not only that there is no single way to be a lesbian but that our understanding of the meanings behind sexual identity labels can evolve quite radically over short periods. Interpreting these shifts demands close attention to the relationship between behavior and how that behavior is spoken and written about, both in public and in private.

Hearing how my students view their own sexuality and how they react to cultural artifacts from the gay and lesbian past underscores this point about the generational specificity of sexual attitudes. I once taught a course on gay and lesbian fiction that began with novels published after World War II. "Couldn't we have started with some more queer positive books?" a lesbian complained. I tried hard to explain that having what she would consider a "queer positive" outlook had been virtually impossible in the 1950s, when gay courage consisted in arriving at some sort of brazen or apologetic (but hardly confident) acceptance of desires almost no one would admit to in public.

I'm not sure she got the message, but then I often doubt that I fully grasp how sex and sexuality have changed for people coming of age in an era affected by positive developments like much greater visibility for lesbians and gays, as well as by negative ones like the AIDS epidemic. Student, writer, and AIDS activist Barry Paddock captures the texture

During World War II, many American women secured work in heavy industry that once would have been considered too dangerous, dirty, and difficult—in short, too "manly"—for women. Today, American women work in scores of positions which once would have been considered unsuitable for them. Such social changes necessarily affect both personal and collective attitudes about gender.

of his gay cultural surroundings in a wonderful slice-of-life piece called "Sex Stories," an excerpt from his zine *Domestic Bliss*:

> Louis doesn't read long books, he watches *90210*, designs club passes and clothes, subscribes to *Sassy*, isn't out to his parents, gets more money from his parents than me, and is intrigued and terrified by my activism. And sometimes it feels like he's everything I could ever need.
>
> • • • • •
>
> Lying in bed I say, "I think I'm falling . . . falling into something with you, I'm not sure what." I'm hedging.
>   "I'm not sure about that," he says.
>
> • • • • •
>
> One night he puts his finger inside my ass. It just burns uncomfortably inside. But afterwards my whole body tingles, each cell is delighted, I feel different than before, older, better, more in the world. I felt like this once before: I was ten years old and at Christmas Eve mass, praying feverishly, and then my body tingled and I was convinced that God had just reached down and touched me.
>
> We get tested together. We are negative.
>
> • • • • •
>
> One weekend I have fun. I am at a party in Brooklyn and talk and joke and flirt without trying. Me and some friends take a cab back to Manhattan. This guy Walter invites me up. We kiss; he has sexy arms. He says, "Here, this will be easier," and pulls out the futon. We suck briefly and use our hands a lot and take a shower together. While he is sucking me I look down and think, it looks like a porn movie. I try to sleep afterwards but I am so hyper that I leap from the bed, say goodbye, run home, and write all night.
>   I haven't written since splitting up with Louis.
>
> • • • • •
>
> I run into Louis. "Did you know it was World AIDS Day last week?" Yes, he knew from the news. "Did you see the ACT UP guy interrupting the President's speech?" Yes, he'd seen it.

• • • • •

On Valentine's Day, Tom, Laura, Dennis, Jason Reed and I give lacy valentines to the Board of Ed's AIDS Advisory Council, who are formulating . . . homophobic, abstinence-based AIDS curricula. We burst into the room; Jason starts reading aloud the demands printed on the back of the Valentines, while we pass them out. There are no lesbians or gay men and no people living with AIDS or HIV on the AIDS Advisory Council. I hand a valentine with two women kissing to Reverend Faulkner, head of the council. He tears it up and stuffs it in my jacket. I throw the pieces on the table.

• • • • •

One night I call a phone sex line, wondering if maybe this is a way to meet someone....

Hey guys, says a booming voice, *If you're a mid-to-late-30's hot dominant stud into intense long blowjobs, this cock sucker is looking to ease your rock hard cock into explosive ecstasy with my deepthroat.* He sounds a lot like a used car salesman....

I realize I'm probably not going to meet my next lover this way. . . . I decide never to call back because I feel if I do I'll end up spending hundreds of dollars.

Reading these vignettes, I wonder how what we often think of as the primarily bodily experience of sex is affected by new technologies, not to mention new social movements. (Note how Barry reacts to sex with Walter, remarking that it "looks like a porn movie"; he belongs to the first generation for whom detailed familiarity with moving visual images of sexual acts is likely to precede direct experience of them.) Another student whose frank writing about his own bisexual experience made him seem very worldly remarked wistfully that he thought the availability of sexual imagery made sex less special than it was in the past. For me, the point is not to romanticize the past, but rather to understand the shifts in sexual culture that are happening all the time.

Within a given generation, ethnicity, race, and class affect sexuality in powerful ways. A key figure who has made this point repeatedly, especially during the feminist sexuality debates of the early 1980s, is Chicana lesbian writer Cherríe Moraga. Moraga has argued that her sexuality owes more to Mexican ideas of male-female relations that she absorbed in childhood than it does to antipatriarchal feminist theories. Her point, as explained in her essay "A Long Line of Vendidas," is not that her sexuality is any more influenced by heterosexual models than is that of white lesbians but rather that everybody's sexuality comes from somewhere; to know what it is to be sexual, one must draw on systems of shared, public meanings. According to Moraga, white lesbians are deluding themselves if they claim to have entered a brave new world of revolutionary sexuality completely different from anything they learned in their heterosexual families, while for women of color such a break with the past would mean "risking the loss of some very essential aspects of identity."

White working-class Southern writer Dorothy Allison has similarly commented on ways in which she modeled her lesbian sexuality on heterosexual family models. In a poem from *The Women Who Hate Me*, she writes:

> This side of the wall we are making love
> > teeth, tongue, hands all entwined.
> > You ride hard the edge of my hip, swing
> > me belly tight up to the flat of the wall.
> > I reach back, become a train gaining speed.
> > Just there I hear my sisters, breathing hard
> > their fingers sliding, wide as their eyes.
> > *"Listen." "Just listen to us."*
> > I could, I swear to you, be my mama.
> > You can, I swear, fuck like a man.

> Only a little harder, and I'll break through.
> > My fingers will claw a hole.
> > This wall will come down.
> > We'll reach my sisters' straining fingers.
> > My eyes will fly up like a bird clearing ground
> > and that old grating mysterious engine
> > will shudder, and pound and lift us all clear.

Drawing on Moraga's point about the power of early influences, Chicano sociologist Tomás Almaguer points out that a bicultural identity can mean a split sexual allegiance. He argues that Chicano men who are considered homosexual by North American standards because they are sexually attracted to other men must balance this definition against the Latin American sexual system, which privileges sexual aim over sexual object. In the Latin American system, what defines sexual identity is the act one wants to perform, not the gender of one's sexual partner.

The Latin American system divides the world of male-male encounters into active and passive participants—*activos* and *pasivos* in Mexican terminology. (*Homens* and *bichas* are equivalent terms in parts of Brazil, and other countries have their own expressions.) Activos exhibit an aggressive, penetrating masculinity, while pasivos, who allow themselves to be penetrated, are seen as feminine and devalued. Thus, while any same-sex act or even the first manifestation of same-sex desire is often thought to mark the North American man as "queer," Latin American men who are seen as activos may simply be viewed as "normal men." The pasivos, on the other hand, are more likely to be stigmatized.

This sexual system is often misunderstood by those accustomed to defining sexual identity in terms of sexual object. "How hypocritical," goes the comment. "Those guys go around having sex with other men, yet never admit that they're really gay!" Almaguer's point is that (as was true for 19th-century American women for whom the concept "lesbian" did not yet exist) the category "really gay" has no relevance in this system. It is not a question of better or worse or false or true: both North American and Latin American systems organize sexual identity around gender distinctions, and both privilege some sexual identities at the expense of others. Both systems exclude and stigmatize. What is fundamentally different is what is seen as most important about sexuality— sexual object or sexual aim.

The importance of sexual aim is not unique to the Latin American system. A parallel in some African-American communities is suggested in the Marlon Riggs video *Tongues Untied,* where a black gay man recalls childhood memories of participating in sexual play with neighborhood boys. What made him stand out was that he would willingly "give up booty," whereas the other boys did so only reluctantly, in return for the privilege of playing the dominant role. Another parallel turns up in a sexual system that has been closely studied by scholars interested in establishing or disputing the universality of the modern Euroamerican homosexual identity: that of the classical world of ancient Greece and Rome.

For the ancients, many historians agree, sexuality was not a separate realm of experience, the core of private life; instead it was directly linked to social power and status. People were judged by public behavior, for which there were clear rules; marriage, for instance, was a duty that bore no necessary relationship to erotic satisfaction. Socially powerful males (citizens) enjoyed sexual access to almost all other members of the society (including, in Greece, enslaved males, younger free males, foreigners, and women of all classes). The most significant restriction on their sexual behavior had to do with the types of sexual acts considered appropriate: according to Boswell, a socially superior male might penetrate male inferiors, but if he allowed himself to be penetrated it would be a cause for scandal, and in Rome it could even result in the loss of some of his citizenship rights. "Sexual service [i.e., performing the passive role]," wrote the Roman playwright Seneca, "is an offense for the free born, a necessity for the slave, and a duty for the freedman."

Despite the mythic stature of the poet Sappho as an early lesbian, we have scant record of the sexual opportunities available to women in the ancient world. Officially, they were supposed to be silent in public, and in private life they were sexually defined by patriarchal rules—which of course provides little indication of how women themselves thought about eroticism. Boswell notes that in ancient Rome, "Sexual fulfillment for women was [considered] appropriate only for courtesans, who could, if they wished, have recourse to either males or females."

In Greece, the erotic ideal for the citizen—who was by definition male and not a slave—included relations with a younger male who was not yet old enough for citizenship. Such relationships were expected to coexist with the older partner's marriage; the younger man, in his turn, would probably be married to a woman and take his own young male lover. The older member of the same-sex pair was viewed as a tutor and guide, helping to bring the younger to full adult manhood. Scholars disagree as to whether the age difference was a universal requirement or only a frequent feature of homosexual relations in ancient Greece.

As already noted, essentialists and social constructionists differ as to whether the Greco-Roman sexual system merely reflects a different culture's approach to the universal phenomenon of heterosexual and homosexual orientations or instead demands that the very idea of two mutually exclusive erotic categories defined by sexual object be viewed as a cultural product of the modern West. Constructionists also argue that the Greek and Roman organization of sexual behavior

John K. Hillers took this photograph of the famous Zuni berdache We'wha in 1879. In Native American societies, berdaches were understood as being not men or women but an indeterminate gender that combined elements and characteristics associated with both males and females.

according to categories of social power (that is, the fact that high-status men consistently eroticized their class and gender inferiors) provides strong evidence that "it is not sexuality which haunts society, but society which haunts the body's sexuality," as the scholar Maurice Godelier puts it.

In certain Melanesian cultures, sexual activity between older and younger males is not only viewed positively, as in the Greek case, but is regarded as necessary for proper masculine development. For instance, among the "Sambia," anthropologist Gilbert Herdt's fictitious name for a real tribal group in lowland New Guinea, the essence of masculinity is believed to be present in semen, leading to the requirement that boys perform fellatio on young adult males in order to ingest the vital fluid. Thus, when they reach the age for marrying women, nearly all males in the society have participated in extensive homosexual activity, in both "receptive" and "inserter" roles. Herdt reports that a few continue their same-sex activity even after marriage. The vast majority, however, report a preference for opposite-sex interactions. Anthropologists speculate that women in such societies also have some means of transmitting the essence of femininity, which is thought to reside in blood from menstruation and birth.

Anthropologists refer to groups such as the Sambia as practitioners of institutionalized homosexuality because same-sex behaviors form a recognized, sanctioned, and vigorously promoted facet of their culture. In contrast is the state of affairs in the modern West, where homosexuality is at best reluctantly tolerated by the mainstream. All known societies have some type of opposite-sex institutionalized relations, though the forms vary widely; for instance, among the Sambia intimate or prolonged contact with women is considered very dangerous to masculinity, so heterosexual intercourse is surrounded with a large variety of restrictions.

Indigenous to North America is a complex of institutionalized homosexual practices—the Native American berdache tradition—that differs strikingly from the Melanesian emphasis on same-sex contact as a means of reinforcing masculinity. In many American Indian tribes, a man could be socially redefined as an intermediate gender; in some areas, women could be similarly redefined. The berdache tradition has been traced throughout the southeast, central, and southwest regions of the United States and far south into Latin America.

Typically, a boy destined for adult life as a berdache would display behavior and interests thought appropriate for females; in fact, the cultural definition of berdache status usually focused primarily on transgendered occupational status or preference, rather than sexual behavior. (Some biologically male berdaches apparently married women.) Anthropologist Harriet Whitehead argues that having homosexual sex was understood to follow from a man's adoption of female-like occupational status rather than the other way around. As in the case of the Greeks, the bodily acts of sex seem to have been heavily influenced by social categories.

Sometimes a boy's adoption of the berdache role was forecast by a vision, which again might pose the alternatives of male or female occupations. Berdache adults were understood to possess a sort of mixed identity, sometimes described as "man-woman" or "not-man, not-woman"; in some areas, they were given special duties not normally performed by either men or women. The berdache's social status was higher in some tribes than in others, but in all cases societies sanctioned the contributions of members who did not fit into a strict male-female dichotomy and whose sexual practices could vary accordingly. This flexible attitude earned the disdain of early European observers, who expressed arrogant contempt for what they saw as "effeminacy," "lewdness," and the "nefarious practices" of "sodomites." (The word *berdache* itself is not of American Indian origin but derives from the French for "male prostitute.")

Many examples of American Indian women adopting traditional masculine roles have also been noted. As Harriet Whitehead has observed, "With appropriate circumstances or encouragement, some women consistently cultivated male skills from an early age. . . . if successful in their actions, [they] were honored by the community as a man would be." In her poem "Beloved Women," American Indian lesbian writer and anthropologist Paula Gunn Allen movingly evokes one such

warrior woman figure, even as she speculates on the difficulty of interpreting her experience from a modern perspective:

> It is not known if those
> who warred and hunted on the plains
> chanted and hexed in the hills
> divined and healed in the mountainsgazed and walked beneath the seas
> were Lesbians
> It is never known
> if any woman was a Lesbian
> so who can say that
> she who shivering drank
> warm blood beneath wind-blown moons
> slept tight to a beloved of shininghair
> curled as a smile within crescent arms
> followed her track deep into secret woods
> dreamed other dreams. . . .

From the very early days of Europeans' presence on the North
American continent, American Indian groups came under attack as the
colonizers sought control over ever widening territories. This threat was
cultural as well as physical, and in the second half of the 19th century
the onslaught intensified, legitimized by a white racist ideology that saw
native peoples as doomed to extinction by the laws of social evolution.
The tribal lifeways that had sustained women's high-prestige occupations—and with them, the identity of a "mixed" being, an intermediate
gender, a "not-man, not-woman"—were forcibly modified or erased.

Yet Native Americans refused to vanish. They fought not only for
physical survival but to maintain cultural traditions without which that
survival would be meaningless or even impossible. Will Roscoe, who
researched the life of the noted 19th-century Zuni berdache We'wha,
has written of the evolution of the berdache into a modern gay role, as
Zuni boys who formerly might have become berdaches ceased to adopt
women's dress around the middle of this century. Many of them, he says,
moved to Gallup, New Mexico, took up employment regarded as
women's work, and began to look and act like gay men of the time. In
an article in *OUT/LOOK* magazine in the summer of 1988, he further

commented:

> [In] my conversations and dialogues over the past four years with gay and
> lesbian American Indians[,] I found that some knew about the berdache as
> a living tribal tradition, while others have learned about the role the same
> way I have—through research. But all affirmed a continuity between the
> berdache tradition and their own lives as gay Indians today.

It is fascinating to speculate that Indians in the transition from traditional berdache to urban gay might have felt some affinity with underground, largely white gay culture in the pre-Stonewall decades, precisely because of their own familiarity with the struggle to sustain cultural practices in the face of crushing opposition. Would white gays have recognized the same connection? The possibility suggests the importance for all sexually marginalized groups of learning from the ways in which different cultures organize sexual interactions, rather than holding up a dominant mode (like the Euroamerican focus on sexual object) as a lens through which to view everyone's sexuality. The ability of white gays to learn from the berdache tradition would depend not only on the former group's ability to reject common racist attitudes but on its willingness to discard preconceptions about sexual identity, at least enough to empathize with a way of being gay that has its roots in indigenous traditions.

Thus, to restate the argument with which I began this chapter, even within the borders of the United States, "gay" experiences and communities are far from monolithic. To focus only on whom one has sex with—rather than, for instance, on who is most emotionally important (as in the lesbian continuum model), which acts one performs (as in the Latin American sexual system), or how sexual identity in relation to biological sex might be modified by choice of occupation and dress (as in the berdache tradition)—assigns a place of privilege to a dominant contemporary perspective on sexuality that distorts the self-understanding of many modern Americans who have known same-sex passion. When taken as a guide to understanding sexuality in other times and places, that perspective leads to even more confusion.

What do these cross-cultural comparisons say about possible

answers to the causal question? Nothing conclusive, for as essentialists like John Boswell are quick to argue, the evidence can be interpreted to mean that one is simply looking at different cultural responses to an underlying same-sex orientation. In the case of practitioners of broadly institutionalized homosexuality, perhaps the "real" homosexuals are the minority who consistently prefer same-sex relations even when heterosexual contacts are available.

At the very least, however, the lack of interest with which many cultures view sexual object-choice should lead us to be suspicious of the Euroamerican obsession with that particular dimension of desire and behavior. It should forestall any snap judgment on whether attraction to one gender or the other can plausibly be viewed as a universal—perhaps biologically rooted—fact about people.

Another way to make the point is: if a fixed orientation toward the same or opposite sex were really embedded in each and every developing human being, wouldn't more cultures build their sexual systems around it? To ask this social constructionist question is not to deny the power that homosexual and heterosexual identities and desires hold for people living in Euroamerican cultures nor to support the oppressive notion that bisexuality is somehow more advanced than unidirectional orientation. It is only to note the workability of other modes of organizing sexual interaction and thereby to suggest that the popular view of sex as a self-evident primal urge leaves much unexplained.

Cross-cultural comparisons underline the strong connection between attitudes toward homosexuality and a given culture's understanding of gender. (Gender, in this usage, indicates the social interpretation placed on biological sex differences. All cultures attribute great significance to male-female distinctions, but specific notions of what is involved in being male or female vary widely.) In some cultures where boundaries between male and female are rigidly maintained, same-sex behavior is seen as gender transgression—not quite being a "proper" man or woman. Certainly this has been true of Euroamerican culture, and late-19th-century and early-20th-century explanations of homosexuality often viewed it as a case of gender mismatch: a female soul in a male body, or vice versa.

Although gender identity and sexual conduct are often closely linked, the way in which "gender" is defined and understood varies widely from one culture to another. In Suriname, South America, for example, women known as mati *engage in sexual relations with other women but also maintain relationships with men. In the former West African state of Dahomey, women—like the warriors pictured here—were permitted to marry, and children born to one were regarded as belonging to the other as well.*

On the other hand, strict distinctions are also compatible with institutionalized same-sex contact as a way of instilling or reinforcing the "proper" gender identity, as in ancient Greco-Roman culture or among the Sambia. As Will Roscoe has argued about the Zuni, a less rigid view of gender that recognizes maleness or femaleness as an acquired identity built upon a foundation of anatomical sex may make room for a special gender category that combines elements of both maleness and femaleness. This, in turn, may pave the way for same-sex behavior.

While most cultures seem to have some notion of correspondence between an appropriate gender identity and sexual conduct, which aspect of sex is emphasized, or even what gets counted as sexual, is highly variable. Thus, in the Latin American sexual system, a "proper man" can engage in same-sex relations so long as he takes the dominant role, while the American 19th-century practice of passionate female friendship allowed middle-class women to combine conventional marriages with same-sex relationships of a type that would later be redefined as deviant.

The small South American nation of Suriname, a former Dutch colony, provides another example of tolerance for same-sex behavior that does not conflict with prevailing gender norms. Women known as *mati* or *matisma* in the local language, Sranan Tongo, enter into sexual relations with other women but may simultaneously or subsequently maintain relationships with men with whom they often have children. The same-sex pairings are frequently intergenerational, with the older woman exacting unconditional devotion in return for her attentions, presents, and the teaching she provides to her young lover. Gloria Wekker, who has written on this subject, connects the mati to reported female homosexuality in the West African regions from which the ancestors of the Surinamese women were probably taken as slaves. For instance, in Dahomey two women could marry, and children born to one would be regarded as belonging to the other as well.

The example of the mati raises questions implicit throughout this chapter: can female same-sex relationships be adequately understood as parallels to male same-sex relationships? If attitudes toward homosexuality are seen as being closely related to attitudes toward gender, what is to be made of the fact that male-female is an asymmetrical pairing— that women and men do not generally have equal power or truly complementary roles in most societies?

It follows from this power imbalance that males and females within a single culture may be expected to desire in very different ways and that their gender "transgressions" may also be treated differently. So, for instance, an American "tomboy" girl may be tolerated or even admired, while a "sissie" boy gets mercilessly mocked, reflecting the fact that traditionally male qualities are prized and traditionally female traits devalued. The point is that just as one cannot assume that culturally specific categories can explain everyone's sexuality, so an analysis of one gender's same-sex (or opposite-sex) experience will not necessarily furnish adequate insight into the seemingly parallel experiences of the other gender. Yet all too often male observers—social constructionists and essentialists alike—behave as if studying male sexuality were the same thing as learning about sexuality in general.

Though the discussion in this chapter has focused on same-sex behavior, my examples suggest a number of ways in which societies motivate opposite-sex behavior. A remark recently made by Gina Kolata, coauthor of the much-touted *Sex in America: A Definitive Survey*, which focuses overwhelmingly on heterosexual behavior, seems appropriate here: "We [the authors] were trying to make people think about sex in an entirely different way. We all have this image, first presented by Freud, of sex as a riderless horse, galloping out of control. What we are saying here is that sex is just like any other social behavior: people behave the way they are rewarded for behaving."

As for same-sex behavior, this chapter has shown that it, too, is often socially rewarded; the crushing intolerance of modern European and American sexual systems is far from universal. Yet the persistence of same-sex passion in the face of that very intolerance provides strong motivation for looking to causal theories that explain orientation as inborn.

Such theories, however, present two major problems. They assume a biological basis for an aspect of the modern Euroamerican sexual system that has little meaning in many other cultures. And they assume, as well, precisely the sort of direct link between biological sex and gendered behaviors that feminists have long questioned. They assume, in other words, that biological sex is destiny; that men and women are so intrinsically unalike that something in a person's brain or genes or hormones can unerringly distinguish male from female (despite vast cultural variations in the qualities attributed to each gender) and spark an attraction to one but not the other. But what, exactly, is it in maleness or femaleness that orientation is supposed to orient people to?

Perhaps what we believe about the biological versus the social "realness" of homosexuality ultimately rests on what we believe about the biological versus the social basis of gender. But before investigating this proposition, we need to consider how the modern Euroamerican sexual identities encompassed by the terms "homosexual" and "heterosexual" emerged and how previous generations have attempted to explain them—through accounts that have some surprising features in common with current causal theories.

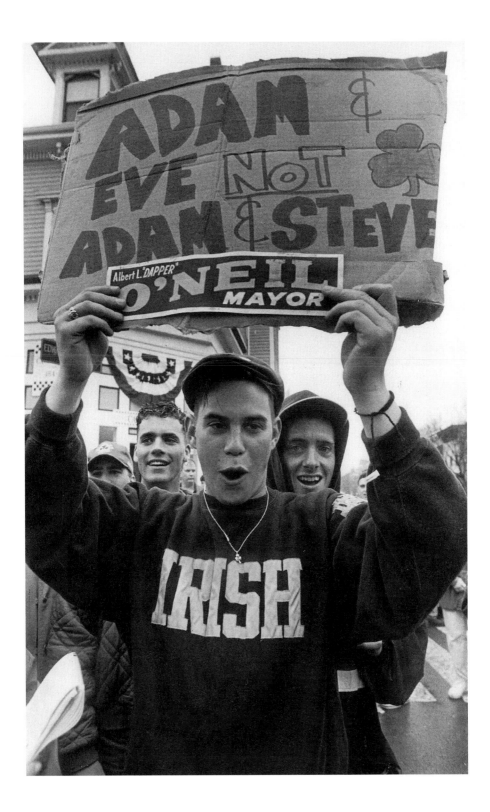

3

The Marriage of Science and Sex and the Birth of Modern Sexual Identities

The slogan displayed by this young Irish-American protester, as a gay and lesbian rights parade passes through his South Boston neighborhood in March 1990, attempts to justify homophobia by appealing to a fundamentalist interpretation of Scripture implying that heterosexual sex for procreational purposes is the natural order of things.

EARLY ATTEMPTS TO EXPLAIN the cause of sexual orientation evolved in tandem with, and contributed to, the emergence of the modern Euroamerican sexual identities of homosexual and heterosexual. Understanding the former—the objective of this chapter—requires some familiarity with historians' arguments concerning the latter.

I have shown that female and male same-sex behaviors are not necessarily mirror images of one another and cannot always be understood using the same interpretive framework. Historians of male and female homosexuality typically take somewhat different approaches to their topic. Scholars concerned with gay men often focus on reports of specific sexual acts and the subcultures built around them, while those studying lesbians tend to concentrate more on intimate, eroticized relationships that under particular circumstances received a sexual definition.

This difference in emphasis raises the question of underlying assumptions. Is there an implication that a lesbian is somehow a less inherently sexual person than a gay man? Or is that idea just a holdover from a sexist gender ideology that restrains and represses female sexuality? Is she perhaps *differently* sexual, responding to gender-specific notions of the erotic? If so, is there any point in seeking to use the same models to understand both male and female homosexuality, or should we conclude that (to borrow the title of a popular book addressed to heterosexuals) "men are from Mars, women are from Venus," and that there is no point in lumping apples and oranges together? These questions cannot be answered definitively but deserve notice because they keep cropping up in current attempts to explain sexual orientation. They also point to the difficulty of constructing a single account of the emergence of gay male and lesbian identities.

Scholars disagree as to the exact time frame in which the modern male homosexual identity emerged, with some tracing it as far back as the late 17th century. There is a general agreement, however, that by the mid-to-late 19th century this new identity was in place and looked quite different from earlier ways of organizing and understanding same-sex behavior. The consolidation of a lesbian identity is thought to have occurred somewhat later. Class and culture played important roles in shaping the new identities of both women and men. There is evidence that many middle- and upper-class white American women were slower to relinquish the tradition of sexually diffuse romantic friendship than were working-class women, and many class-privileged couples continued to present themselves to the world as respectably nonsexual companions well into the mid-20th century. During the Jazz Age that preceded the stock market crash of 1929, Harlem was home to a distinctive African-American lesbian and gay subculture that provided social support to "B.D. women" and

Dr. Magnus Hirschfeld founded the Institute of Sexology in Berlin. Hirschfeld was an early member of the Scientific Humanitarian Committee, the first gay emancipation organization. Among its other activities, the committee published the "Yearbook for Intermediate Sexual Types," a compendium of material about homosexuality.

"sissy men."

Despite the universality of institutionalized heterosexuality (the social promotion and regulation of particular sorts of opposite-sex relations), heterosexuality as an identity, a way of describing the self, is also a distinctly modern phenomenon. Historian Jonathan Ned Katz has placed the debut of the "modern American heterosexual" in the years 1892–1900, when medical and scientific authorities first began to use the term, paired with its opposite, "homosexual."

The pairing represented a new, official demarcation between "normality" and "deviance," categories that in effect require and depend on one another. It also signaled a new, medically sanctioned notion that being sexual with the opposite sex was a healthy component of both masculinity and femininity, and a corresponding, though gradual, shift away from the previous Euroamerican emphasis on procreation (making babies) as the be-all and end-all of opposite-sex pairing. Like the newly emergent homosexual, the heterosexual had been provided with a complex of new meanings and values to attach to a familiar configuration of bodies.

The homosexuality-heterosexuality duality was not created by science alone; to explain it fully, one must examine a range of other factors, including the growth of urban environments, changes in family structure, the evolution of capitalist economic relations, and attempts by same-sex lovers themselves to make a social space for the enactment of their desires. But the disciplines of psychoanalysis, psychiatry, and sexology did play a vital role in the emergence of these identities, as men of science (and *men* they were indeed, in that highly sexist era) devoted themselves to explaining sexual desire as a key to the mysteries of the human personality. Their efforts included description and classification of an ever-expanding list of sexual types; attempted causal explanations in terms of biology or psychological developmental sequences; and, in many cases, efforts to cure conditions they deemed unhealthy.

These activities had a curious double-edged effect. On the one hand, while the "experts" believed they were simply discovering the objective truths of sexual "nature," with the benefit of hindsight we can see that they often enshrined their own and the society's prejudices. As French thinker Michel Foucault observed in *The History of Sexuality* (perhaps the most influential text of social constructionism), in making rules for what could be considered "truth," these scholars founded a branch of knowledge that was simultaneously an instrument of power. On the other hand, they fashioned a tool that could, on occasion, be used effectively to combat prejudice and stigma—as it was, for instance, by gay sexologist and homophile campaigner Magnus Hirschfeld.

This historical ambiguity—sex as the prisoner of science versus science as sex's rescuer—has never been resolved. It accounts for some of the intensity of debates between social constructionists, who, like Foucault, have often stressed the sinister role of science, and essentialist advocates of biological research, who hope that scientific understanding can help demystify and destigmatize same-sex behavior.

In the second half of the 19th century, scientists and scholars in Germany and Austria helped develop influential theories of sexuality in general and homosexuality in particular. Simultaneously, Germany was the scene of the first public campaigns for homosexual emancipation, which by the turn of the century had flowered into Dr. Magnus Hirschfeld's tireless campaign to promote the scientific study of sex.

In Psychopathia Sexualis, *Austrian psychiatrist Richard von Krafft-Ebing characterized sex as a "nauseous disease"and homosexuality as a fundamental sign of degeneration.*

Hirschfeld chaired the Scientific Humanitarian Committee in its fight to repeal Paragraph 175, the German sodomy law. A homosexual himself, he combined work on behalf of same-sex lovers with dedication to greater understanding of all sexualities, eventually becoming an organizer of the World League for Sexual Reform. His famous Institute for Sexology in Berlin was destroyed by the Nazis in 1933. Meanwhile, Dr. Sigmund Freud of Vienna was formulating his psychoanalytic theories of the sexual unconscious. The German-speaking world remained at the forefront of both theoretical innovations and antirepressive campaigns until the rise of fascism, with its virulent persecution of homosexuals, other sexual nonconformists, and what the Nazis called "Jewish science."

In England, Havelock Ellis wielded major influence over medical opinion, even though his *Studies in the Psychology of Sex* was banned as filthy in his native land after the 1897 publication of the first volume, *Sexual Inversion,* and had to be brought out by a U.S. publisher. Like Hirschfeld, Ellis was prominent in the World League and gained an international reputation.

In the wake of World War II, American scientists took the lead in sexological research. Maverick American sex researcher Alfred Kinsey challenged received wisdom about sexual orientation with his revelations of widespread same-sex activity in the general adult population and his refusal to classify the people he studied as exclusively straight or gay. The ostentatiously heterosexual husband–wife team of William Masters and Virginia Johnson developed a laboratory approach to the scientific study of sex, observing "live sex acts" by both heterosexual and homosexual couples.

Many early sexological accounts of homosexuality saw it as an inborn, biologically based condition marked by a reversal or inversion of "natural" gender characteristics: the homosexual, in this formulation, represented an intermediate gender category, a third sex. K. H. Ulrichs, an early campaigner for homosexual liberation who influenced later theoretical developments with writings he began to publish in Germany in the 1860s, expounds this view in the following passage. "Urning" or "Uranian" was Ulrichs's term for same-sex-oriented men, and "Dionian" for those attracted to the opposite sex:

There is a class of born Urnings, a class of individuals who are born with the sexual drive of women and have male bodies. They are a subspecies of men whose Uranian love is congenital. . . . By congenital is meant sexual, organic and mental inheritance, not an inherited disease and not such inheritances as pyromania, kleptomania and alcoholism, but rather an inheritance such as Dionians receive in their sexual drives towards women and vice versa.

A landmark event in the development of the new sexual science was the 1886 publication of Richard von Krafft-Ebing's *Psychopathia Sexualis: A Medico-Forensic Study, with Especial Reference to the Antipathic Sexual Instinct*. A professor of psychiatry at the University of Vienna, Krafft-Ebing set out to study sex offenders from a medical point of view. His work excited unexpected interest, and he continued to publish ever larger editions, elaborating a complicated classification system for presumed disorders—including four categories of lesbians, each one to be distinguished by a combination of physical, sexual, and social traits.

The theme of degeneration—homosexuality as a progressive form of insanity—was a significant strand in late-19th-century efforts to describe the so-called contrary sexual impulse. Bearing this in mind, one can see how Ulrichs's theory of an innate homosexuality that was not diseased or deficient was for his day startlingly progressive and affirming of same-sex-oriented men, despite its reliance on a model that solidified "proper" gender characteristics and explained homosexuality as a reversal of them. Magnus Hirschfeld also thought that homosexuals were what he called an intermediate sex and used this idea as an argument for tolerance.

Far-fetched attempts to correlate bodily form and appearance with mental characteristics were a staple of 19th-century science, and sexologists made many efforts to relate body type and homosexual behavior. Same-sex erotic orientation in men was commonly attributed to "feminine" body structure—the intersex model again, here transplanted from Ulrich's notion of sexual drive to the physique of the affected individual. Sex differentiation was prized as a sign of advanced development, the opposite of degeneration; homosexuals, supposedly more like the opposite sex than their "normal" counterparts, were held to be at a lower level of development.

Influenced by the sexologists' prodigious efforts to bring sexuality under the same scientific scrutiny to which 19th-century science routinely subjected other "natural" phenomena, Sigmund Freud took a further step in consolidating our modern notion of sexuality as the hidden truth of both the individual psyche and of civilization itself. By the century's second decade, his writings were already being trans-

"It is one of the obvious injustices of social life that the standards of culture should demand the same behavior in sexual life from everyone," wrote Sigmund Freud, the founder of psychoanalysis. Although Freud believed that homosexuality should not be considered a vice or illness, not even something "to be ashamed of," he did regard it as a "certain arrest of sexual development."

lated and popularized for a North American audience that quickly absorbed, at least on a superficial level, his notions of infantile sexuality and familial sexual dramas.

While some of his disciples were blatant homophobes, Freud himself offered a complex account of the psychic roots of sexual orientation that differs in noteworthy and potentially progressive ways from biologically based inversion theories. His theory is psychodynamic (process oriented) and as such represents more of an effort to account for the emergence of a mental disposition than did theories that simply invoked an unknown biological principle. (However, the ambiguous biological assumptions behind the notion of "drives" have been the subject of much debate.) The theory states that heterosexuality, as well as homosexuality, requires explanation and cannot simply be posited as a natural result of the imperative for species reproduction. It puts bisexuality at the center of its explanatory apparatus and indeed suggests that at an unconscious level all human beings are bisexual.

In a note added in 1915 to *Three Essays on Sexuality,* which had originally been published 10 years earlier, Freud stated,

> Psychoanalytic research is most decidedly opposed to any attempt at separating off homosexuals from the rest of mankind as a group of a special character. By studying sexual excitations other than those that are manifestly displayed, it has found that all human beings are capable of making a homosexual object-choice and have in fact made one in their unconscious. . . . On the contrary, psychoanalysis considers that a choice of an object independently of its sex—freedom to range equally over male and female objects—as it is found in childhood, in primitive states of society and early periods of history, is the original basis from which, as a result of restriction in one direction or the other, both the normal and the inverted [homosexual] types develop. Thus from the point of view of psychoanalysis the exclusive sexual interest felt by men for women is also a problem that needs elucidating and is not a self-evident fact based upon an attraction that is ultimately of a chemical nature.

Freud's theory implicitly poses an interesting challenge to heterosexuals, since it suggests that their sexual identity is not as monolithic or inevitable as they may have assumed—indeed, that on an unconscious level the straightest of the straight may harbor same-sex desire. In contrast, a biological theory claiming that people are by nature oriented in a single, fixed direction promises both heterosexuals and homosexuals the comfort (or claustrophobia) of assuming that their identities are rock solid, that the closets of their unconscious harbor no skeletons.

As early as 1903, Freud had expressed his belief that what he called a perverse orientation should not be treated either as a sickness or as a criminal matter. Much later, in 1930, he would sign a statement urging the decriminalization of homosexual acts. He was consistent in his position, upholding the right of homosexuals to become psychoanalysts if they so desired, over the objection of his colleagues.

Given all this, gay cultural historian Henry Abelove has recently argued, Freud's bad reputation among later generations of gay rights advocates stemmed less from his actual views than from the ways in which his work was interpreted—or subverted—by homophobic American analysts. Their "scientific" perspective on homosexuality included the assumption that same-sex orientation was indeed an illness, as it was officially deemed by the American Psychiatric Association in 1952. This diagnostic classification was abolished only in 1973 as the result of a well-organized campaign both inside and outside the organization.

Having invented the disease—according to Dr. Charles Socarides, homosexual relationships were associated with "destruction, mutual defeat, exploitation…, oral-sadistic incorporation, aggressive onslaughts, attempts to alleviate anxiety, and a pseudo-solution to the aggressive libidinal urges which dominate and torment the individual"— American doctors traced its origins to distant fathers and over-involved mothers. They then offered psychoanalysis as a cure. Ridiculous as their prescriptions now appear to most people, notions of homosexuality as psychopathology and attempts to blame it on family relationships have certainly not receded from popular consciousness. Many older gay men and lesbians still vividly recall their years of subjection to what Martin Duberman has aptly called "the tortures of the talking cure." And Dr. Socarides, whose own son is openly gay, continues his homophobic crusade through an organization called the National Association for

Research and Therapy of Homosexuality.

This shameful history does much to explain post-Stonewall gays' widespread mistrust of psychological theories of sexual orientation. Remember, too, that the tortures inflicted on gays in the United States and elsewhere in the name of psychological science sometimes went far beyond talk to physical assaults in the form of lobotomy and "chemical castration." Gene researcher Dean Hamer reports the case, apparently from the 1950s, of a man who was arrested in California on a sodomy charge and given the choice of jail or a psychiatric hospital. Having chosen the latter, he was subjected to a brain operation that involved drilling holes in his skull and left him paralyzed on one side of his body for several months. Following his release from the hospital, he tried hard to go straight and even got married. He eventually decided that the effort would not work and subsequently built a fulfilling life for himself as an openly gay man.

Although Freud himself would have been appalled by such abuse in the name of treatment, as the most influential figure in modern psychology he tends to be associated with the sins of later generations of analysts and psychiatrists. While his expressed position during his lifetime placed him on the side of the sexual reformers, he in fact clashed with the arch-reformer Magnus Hirschfeld over the latter's attachment to the intermediate sex theory. Their encounter provides an interesting example of the long-standing rivalry between the fields of biology and psychology in the race to explain homosexuality, a competition that has continued into the present. Indeed, the gap left by the debunking of blatantly homophobic psychological theories probably does a good deal to help explain the current popularity of biological approaches.

It has been argued that Hirschfeld may have been reluctant to countenance alternative theories because a biological argument was key to his strategy in various public campaigns for greater understanding of homosexuality, in particular his efforts against the sodomy law. This German debate intriguingly foreshadows current discussion in the United States about the possible usefulness of biological research in advancing legal remedies against homophobic discrimination.

One commentator, writing in the *German Medical Weekly* in 1924, reasoned:

> If homosexual intercourse, as a general rule, is simply the expression of a deep-seated constitutional disposition, then the state scarcely has any cause to make this a punishable offense. Assuming the above assumption to be correct, then the essential determinant of criminality, i.e. guilt, would be lacking, for someone who acts simply as an expression of a deep-seated constitutional disposition does not act in a blameworthy way.

The argument made no headway, and within the decade the Nazis came to power, sealing the fate of the sexual reform movement. In 1933, a few months after Adolf Hitler became chancellor, the Nazi Committee Against the Un-German Spirit burned the library and archives of the Institute for Sexology. Its founder, Hirschfeld—who as a Jew, a homosexual, and a leftist would have stood no chance of survival in his native country—died in exile in France. As late as the early 1960s, Hirschfeld's reasoning was still being rejected in his homeland: the German draft penal code of 1962 dismissed arguments for decriminalizing homosexuality with the comment, "If the viewpoint underlying this assumption [that what is 'natural' or constitutionally determined should not be penalized] were accepted, society would have to accept and honour every variety of human nature as natural, no matter how degenerate." Hirschfeld's advocacy of the right to same-sex love was only tardily vindicated at the end of that decade, when the law was liberalized.

Like so many of his colleagues on the continent, British sexologist Havelock Ellis saw "sexual inversion" as innate. While he called for the decriminalization and destigmatization of homosexual behavior, he also played an influential role in bringing lesbians under the discipline of sexological definitions. He distinguished between the "true invert," who was congenitally of the "intermediate sex," and women who he thought were potentially heterosexual but susceptible to lesbian seduction.

In a striking instance of the many cases in which gay men and lesbians have tried to enlist the apparently alienating and objectifying theories of sexology in their own liberation struggles, English novelist Radclyffe Hall adopted the sexologists' invert theory to explain the des-

The experience of British psychologist Havelock Ellis is indicative of the obstacles that the first scientific researchers into sexual behavior faced. Sexual Inversion, *the second volume of Ellis's groundbreaking seven-volume* Studies in the Psychology of Sex, *was banned as pornographic after a bookseller who sold the item was brought to trial on obscenity charges.*

tiny of her lesbian main character, Stephen Gordon, in *The Well of Loneliness*, perhaps the most famous lesbian novel of all time. Because of its daringly frank depiction of a woman-loving woman, the novel became the target of British censors, was the subject of an obscenity trial, and later emerged as an icon for generations of lesbians who looked to it as one of the few print sources that reflected something of their own erotic lives. While post-Stonewall lesbians tended to reject the book for its self-hating approach to the female body and its lugubrious embrace of tragedy as the inevitable lesbian fate, historian Esther

Dr. Alfred Kinsey was the most innovative of American researchers into sexual behavior. Kinsey argued that it was misleading to define homosexuality and heterosexuality as mutually exclusive categories and proposed that sexual behavior be understood as proceeding along a continuum.

Newton has pointed out that at least the invert theory had the virtue of offering an explicitly sexual account of lesbianism, at a point when women were not often thought to be active agents of desire.

American sex researcher Alfred Kinsey rejected the role of border patrol guard between the domains of the normal and abnormal that earlier generations of sexologists had so eagerly embraced. One of his most controversial and startling findings had to do with the frequency of male homosexual behavior. In *Sexual Behavior in the Human Male,* published in 1948, he estimated that only half of the white male population was exclusively heterosexual throughout adult life.

The figure has often been disputed, with skeptics quick to point out that the 18,000 intimate sexual case histories Kinsey and his coworkers eventually compiled did not come from a random sample of the adult population and may have been weighted in favor of less usual behaviors. Still, his work provided a benchmark, the point of origin for the almost magical figure of 10 percent that is still frequently cited as the percentage of any population assumed to be gay. (Kinsey himself did not quite make this claim; rather, he said that 10 percent of the adult white males he surveyed had spent three or more years engaging in predominantly homosexual activity.)

In keeping with his discovery that sexual behavior was much more variable than had been supposed, Kinsey rejected the usual sexological assumption that such behavior translates into types of individuals. "It would encourage clearer thinking on these matters," he maintained, "if persons were not characterized as heterosexual or homosexual, but as individuals who have had certain amounts of heterosexual experience and certain amounts of homosexual experience." In order to calculate these amounts, he devised his famous seven-point scale (zero through six). A Kinsey rating of six would be someone who reported only homosexual behavior and feelings; a three would report being equally drawn to the same and the opposite sex; a zero would be exclusively heterosexual. Ones, twos, fours, and fives would represent an unevenly balanced mixture of inclinations to both the same and the opposite sex.

Critics have since pointed out a number of problems with this scale, such as its assumption that vigorous interest in one sex means slight interest in the other. What about the person who might be vigorously attracted to both men and women in equal proportions? He or she would receive the same Kinsey three as someone who exhibited faint but balanced interest in both sexes. The scale also ignores the fact that some individuals may seek very different satisfactions in their relations with partners of their own sex from what they want in an opposite-sex partner. Despite its shortcomings, the Kinsey scale was unprecedented in its effort to represent gradations of attraction rather than fixed, dualistic identities—thus opening up the possibility that, in Jeffrey Weeks's words, "homosexuality might not be a unitary phenomenon with a single causative explanation."

Enormously influential in the 1960s, husband-wife sex researchers William Masters and Virginia Johnson saw themselves as Kinsey's heirs. Their detailed studies of the physiology of human sexual behavior established as scientific fact the importance of the clitoris in female arousal and the phenomenon of the multiple orgasm, causing a revolution in popular awareness that women's reports of their own experience had been unable to bring about. They made masturbation almost respectable. They also reported in a 1979 study that lesbians and gay males were appreciably better at sexually pleasing their partners than were heterosexuals, remarking rather nervously that such a finding might become "an effective recruiting argument for lesbianism."

Their work had contradictory effects. They used the prestige of science to normalize and reinforce both gender differences and heterosexuality. Viewing the point of their research as helping heterosexuals to get along better, they shrank from any notion that some women might be better off in same-sex relationships. In 1972 William Masters explained the growth of sex therapy by saying, "A man and a woman need each other more now than ever before. People need someone to hold on to. Once they had the clan but now they only have each other."

Yet their findings were put to work by people with other goals in mind. For instance, the new emphasis on clitoral sexuality gave feminists a powerful argument in favor of a woman's right to pleasure on her own terms—even as the narrow focus on physiology implied a unified model of erotic satisfaction that threatened to impose its own tyranny.

The husband-and-wife team of Virginia Johnson and William Masters succeeded Kinsey as the best-known American sex researchers. Among their more interesting findings was that almost all of the individuals they studied—regardless of their behavior or self-identification—reported that they had sexual fantasies involving members of the same sex.

Ultimately, the precise content of Masters and Johnson's work, as well as that of other "sexperts," may have been less significant than the way in which their research further extended the domain of sexology—the presumption that science is the best way to know and define the erotic.

Three overarching themes connect successive phases of the eccentric yet remarkably stable union between science and sex. The first is the idea of "the natural"; the second, assumptions about human reproduction as the grounding principle of sexuality. The third is our old friend, the causal question.

Notions of nature and the natural haunt current thinking on sexual behavior in general and sexual orientation in particular. What, after all, is the cute but puerile slogan "God made Adam and Eve, not Adam and Steve" if not an appeal to the idea of nature as delineated by Judeo-Christian doctrine? In response to long-standing notions that homosexuality is a "crime against nature" (language that has actually been used in anti-sodomy statutes), gay rights advocates have often been quick to assert that same-sex love is indeed very natural.

I can cite an example from my own writing. In a poem of mine called "Likeness" that appeared in a lesbian literary magazine in the mid-1970s, I wrote that "love in the mirror" (i.e. love between women) is "only the world's most natural act." There is by now a well established lesbian literary tradition connecting images of female lovers to images of the earth. I frequently find such ideas reflected in student comments and writing. "I just see my sexuality as a very natural thing," one young woman repeated as she tried to explain her evolution from a militantly political bisexuality to a quieter acceptance of her feelings.

It was inevitable that the early sexologists would invoke nature. As scientists they studied processes that, according to Charles Darwin's theory of evolution, related closely to the phenomena of the animal world. They saw themselves as objective observers of what was "out there." Yet their model of nature turned out to be anything but self-evident and neutral. In fact, they had seized hold of a powerful ideological weapon.

The appeal to nature served as a declaration of independence from Christian theology's ancient pronouncements against bodily desires, which had been based on the idea of a radical break between human and animal. Thus the stamp of the natural could validate sexual behavior, removing old shame and stigma. But the natural itself became a new kind of value judgment. Sexologists' descriptions were in reality prescriptions for appropriate behavior, prescriptions that often concealed the authors' own fantasies and fears.

As Jeffrey Weeks points out, "Krafft-Ebing's [definition of sex as] 'natural instinct' which 'with all conquering force and might demands fulfilment' is an image of male sexuality whose natural object was the opposite sex." Carroll Smith-Rosenberg notes that Havelock Ellis's books "reveal a man troubled by changes he could not in principle oppose. Feminism, lesbianism, equality for women, all emerge in Ellis's writings as problematic phenomena. All were unnatural, related in disturbing and unclear ways to increased female criminality, insanity, and hereditary neurosis."

One hundred years after the full emergence of the modern identities of homosexual and heterosexual, we remain ambiguously in thrall to the authority of science as the arbiter of the natural, and in turn to the natural as the standard of the sexually appropriate—assumptions whose consequences will be further examined in the upcoming chapters.

Beliefs about the place of human reproduction in sexual behavior swarm around the concept of the natural like worker bees around their queen, drawing strength from and in turn reinforcing assumptions about the necessary, immutable character of differences between men and women. So old, pervasive, and intertwined are these ideas that even today they serve as instant authorization for distinctions between the normal and the abnormal, the permissible and the perverted. Alternatively, they mark off that which seems mysterious, unexpected, and in need of a causal explanation (same-sex behavior, which does not reproduce the species) from that which is self-evident and self-explanatory (opposite-sex behavior, which does). Because this procreationist prejudice is so common, it requires more detailed examination.

Even as sexology moved further and further away from a direct reliance on baby making to account for and legitimize sexual activity, procreation-related explanations continued to be invoked through their proxy, the eternal pairing of male and female. Such notions took deep root in popular culture, where they still retain a flavor of scientific sanction.

A certain amount of confusion about what science claims to have established has no doubt been due to the scientists' own lack of clarity as they strove to pin down the "instinct" that was supposed to account for sex. Procreation still figured in Krafft-Ebing's theory, and in some of the earliest recorded uses of the term "heterosexual," American doctors actually employed it as a description of abnormal lust that, while direct- ed toward the proper opposite-sex object, was insufficiently anchored in the reproductive urge. Yet notions of sex-as-reproduction too obviously failed to account for nonreproductive opposite-sex behavior as well as

A participant in a gay rights demonstration held in New York City in June 1994 gives her own response to the so-called causal question.

for same-sex behavior. Science soon moved on to less simplistic theories, but popular awareness lagged behind.

In the 1950s, for instance, the adjective "sterile" was often used to call up negative images of homosexuality, as though the mere fact that two individuals did not have the potential to mingle their chromosomes in creating a third was automatic proof of their emotional barrenness. Meanwhile, lyrics to popular tunes reinforced the links between "nature," procreation, and opposite sex lust:

> Let me tell you 'bout the birds and the bees
> And the flowers and the trees
> And the moon up above . . .
> And a thing called love.

A student recently remarked that as a child he never could figure out what "the birds and the bees" meant, since his parents had skipped the euphemisms and given him a no-nonsense explanation of human reproduction. But how many parents explain sexuality to their children in anything but procreationist terms that help reinforce the equation NATURAL SEX = A MAN GETTING A WOMAN PREGNANT?

Contemporary "family values" discourse draws heavily on the legacy of procreationist attitudes, ignoring the obvious facts that many heterosexuals either have no interest in making babies or are physically unable to do so, that many "procreative" acts (rape, for instance) are abusive and antisocial, and that many lesbians and gay men are enthusiastic parents. "God made Adam and Eve" is an appeal not just to nature but to "natural" links between sex and procreation.

As usual, the concept of nature cloaks a value judgment. But those who would like to account for opposite-sex attraction by invoking the reproductive functions of male and female genitalia forget that the genitals do not, in and of themselves, demand to be used in any particular way. In fact, the absence of estrus in human females (meaning that, unlike other mammals, women do not give perceptible signs when they are ready to be impregnated, as animals do when they "go into heat") actually seems to indicate an evolutionary step away from the physiological linkage between genitals and reproduction: women remain sexually active at times of the month when they are unable to conceive.

A more important point is that genital sexuality, like all human behavior, is culturally shaped. Human reproduction occurs not in a framework of instinct but of elaborate and diverse systems of institutionalized heterosexuality, the universality of which arguably suggests that the coming together of men and women might occur much less often if it were not culturally reinforced. On the other hand, exclusively homosexual behavior is fairly rare in most cultures, so same-sex behavior need not get in the way of reproduction (which should end the bewilderment of people who want to know why natural selection has not eliminated gays).

Heterosexual behavior is no less mysterious than homosexual behavior: one body touching another can provide intense pleasure, according to the physiological principles investigated by Masters and Johnson—but that pleasure is already drenched in richly complicated meanings. Notions of the natural, normal, appropriate, virtuous, right, clean, and straight are one set of meanings; notions of the unnatural, the perverse, the abnormal, the illicit, the wicked, wrong, dirty, and bent are another. Depending on the circumstances, either set can incite and enhance the coming together of bodies (the clean is sometimes boring, the perverse extra sexy). Or one set can replace the other, as when stigmatized nonprocreative opposite-sex behavior received the sanction of the new heterosexual identity. Current efforts by some gay people to obtain the stamp of approval of genetics and neuroscience for same-sex orientation appear to be centered on the hope of another such reversal.

Opposite-sex attraction requires an explanation just as much as does same-sex attraction. Yet the causal question was implicit in the very terms in which science first defined the homosexual, in a way that was not true for its nonidentical twin, the heterosexual. Conceived of as a deviation from the expected course of nature, homosexuality was from the beginning the sort of phenomenon of which one could—indeed, practically had to—ask: What causes it? And the question implied the existence of an answer. It did not allow for the notion that there might be many answers. Nor did it admit the possibility that the model of cause-and-effect, with all of its baggage from the physical sciences, its notion of linear trains of events and its lingering hope of prediction and control, is just too simplistic to be useful in explaining complicated human behaviors.

4

After Stonewall

IN 1975, A MAN named Leonard Matlovich was discharged from the U.S. Air Force for being a homosexual. Sergeant Matlovich, a staunch patriot of generally conservative views who had lost his virginity to another man at the age of 30, contested his discharge, generating the first widely publicized gays in the military case. At a hearing to determine whether or not he would be reinstated, witnesses for the defense included prominent sex researchers, one of whom, John Money of the psychohormonal research unit at Johns Hopkins University, testified as to the probable biological roots of sexual orientation.

Leonard Matlovich meets the press in Washington, D.C., in 1987. About his discharge from the U.S. Air Force for homosexuality, Matlovich once said, "They gave me a medal for killing two men, and a discharge for loving one."

This testimony was significant, wrote historian Martin Duberman, not only because it represented a theoretical shift on Money's part (his earlier work had explained homosexuality as the result of socialization, not innate factors) but because it signaled a sea change in Americans' beliefs about the origins of social arrangements. Duberman detected "a general resurgence, a renewed acceptability in our culture, of the belief that biological considerations are the basic ones in any explanation of human behavior." At the time, most gay activists remained aloof from the trend, at least in part, thought Duberman, because of their awareness of the damaging uses to which inaccurate but ideologically potent scientific findings about homosexuality had been put in the past.

Two decades later, biological explanations enjoy ever greater popularity. The mass media ballyhoo the discovery of an "obesity gene," even as observers point out that the fact that Americans are, on average, significantly heavier than they were 10 years ago could not possibly be genetically influenced. A book suggesting that evolution predisposes men to marital infidelity sells like hotcakes, amid protests from feminists. *The Bell Curve* claims that the continued impoverishment of a significant section of the U.S. population is attributable to inherited inferior IQs and that African Americans are, as a group, intellectually less capable than whites; the book is respectfully treated in many quarters despite reams of expert refutation establishing that African Americans and Caucasians are not genetically distinguishable groups, that neither IQ nor any other one-dimensional measurement can be considered a valid description of human intelligence, and that environment has an enormous and often unpredictable impact on the development of genetic potential.

And now there is a "gay gene"—or rather, the promise of one. On July 16, 1993, *Science,* one of the most respected U.S. scientific journals, published an article by Dean Hamer and colleagues entitled "A Linkage Between DNA Markers on the X Chromosome and Male Sexual Orientation." The researchers claimed to have found convincing evidence of the existence of a gene that, in combination with environmental factors, plays a role in sexual orientation for some (not all) gay men. Though often less than accurate, media coverage of the announcement was avid, probably in part because the article's publication coincided with suspense over the pending resolution of President Bill Clinton's fumbled attempt to liberalize official policy on gays in the military. A number of gay activists jumped on the bandwagon. Speaking for the Human Rights Campaign, the nation's largest gay rights organization, Gregory J. King said, "We find the [Hamer] study very relevant, and what's most relevant is that it's one more piece of evidence that sexual orientation is not chosen."

What had taken place to account for the change from 1975, when the majority of gays seemed mistrustful of Money's biological theories in the Matlovich case, to 1993, when many seemed eager to embrace Hamer's genetic research? Part of the answer lies in the fact that lesbians and gay men, like everyone else, have now experienced two decades of exposure to the intellectual climate Martin Duberman identified. At the same time, many lesbians, gays, bisexuals, and self-identified queers have fiercely resisted the rush to biological thinking. Responding to the Hamer findings, Darrell Yates Rist of the Gay and Lesbian Alliance Against Defamation told the *New York Times:*

> I don't think it's an interesting study. Intellectually, what do we gain by finding out there's a homosexual gene? Nothing, except an attempt to identify those people who have it and open them up to all sorts of experimentation to change them.

The publicity given to recent biological research has heightened the tension between essentialists and constructionists, but that tension has deep roots in the history of gay activists' attempts to carve out viable identities and increase the range of freedoms for same-sex-loving people in the post-Stonewall decades of the 1970s and 1980s.

As Duberman stated, members of the early gay liberation movement had good reason to mistrust causal explanations. Many had suffered personally the effects of psychiatric theories that told them they were sick and equated health with conversion to heterosexuality. They wanted no part of it. They responded by turning the tables, labeling as sick, repressive, and damaging the majority's attempt to slot people into ironclad sexual categories. Liberation, they felt, would involve freeing everyone to realize a potential for erotic connection to both genders. In effect, they reclaimed the radical promise of Freud's idea that an exclusive orientation toward same or opposite sex involves repression of an underlying bisexuality. In Dennis Altman's phrase, they advocated "the end of the homosexual"—but, of course, the end of the heterosexual as well.

Poet and activist Martha Shelley forcefully expressed these ideas in an eloquent polemic, "Gay Is Good," that she addressed to straights and published in the underground newspaper *Rat:*

> We Gays are separate from you—we are alien. You have managed to drive your own homosexuality down under the conscious skin of your mind—and to drive us down and out into the gutter of self-contempt. We, ever since we became aware of being gay, have each day been forced to internalize the labels: "I am a pervert, a dyke, a fag, etc." And the days pass, until we look at you out of our homosexual bodies, bodies that have become synonymous and consubstantial with homosexuality, bodies that are no longer bodies but labels; and sometimes we wish we were like you, sometimes we wonder how you can stand yourselves…. We want you to understand what it is to be our kind of outcast—but also to understand our kind of love, to hunger for your own sex…. We will never go straight until you go gay. And because we will not wait, your awakening may be a rude and bloody one.

Rather than seeing lesbians and gay men as a special sexual type, Shelley saw them as the ultimate rebels: "We are men and women who, from the time of our earliest memories, have been in revolt against the sex-role structure and the nuclear family structure."

As the gay movement consolidated, however, this frontal assault on the very notion of boundaries between sexual identities rapidly lost popularity. Gay activists began to argue that gays were a sexual minority deserving of the same rights as other citizens. Instead of tearing down the system, the new goal was to rearrange it, allowing homosexuals to participate on a more equal basis. The shift from a radical liberation perspective to a moderate gay rights argument highlighted a basic philosophic difference that has since reappeared in various forms; currently, it surfaces in debates between "queers" who want to challenge the straight world with the defiant otherness of their sexuality and gays intent on winning a better chance to swim in the mainstream.

In another significant development of the early post-Stonewall years, lesbians increasingly split off from gay men to work exclusively

Many of those who hope for the discovery of a so-called gay gene believe that a genetic explanation for sexual desire might reduce homophobia by demonstrating that gayness is no less "natural" than straightness. Such thinking is overly optimistic about the nature of homophobia. Bigots are infinitely resourceful in finding "justification" for their prejudice, no matter what form it may take.

with women. Lesbian feminists, put off by the sexism of their gay brothers, developed a politics that defined lesbianism as the ultimate refusal of a patriarchal order. According to a manifesto published by Radicalesbians in 1970, "A lesbian is the rage of all women condensed to the point of explosion." Lesbians who shared this analysis drew on the work of heterosexual feminist theorists who had sought to revise patriarchal psychoanalytic models of psychic development to account for women's experiences and the development of gender identity.

According to Nancy Chodorow's *The Reproduction of Mothering*, for a boy raised within the traditional Western nuclear family the attainment of masculine identity requires a sharp break with the first caregiver (presumably the mother) with whom he was emotionally fused in his infancy. The boy in effect must take the position toward her of "I am not you." For a girl, however, experiencing herself as fully female is compatible with retaining strong ties to a powerful woman figure, so there is no sharp break. Adrienne Rich used this theory to argue that lesbianism, as it is based on the early emotional closeness of a girl to her mother, is "a profoundly *female* experience," having little in common with male same-sex attraction. Thus, by a roundabout path, a version of the psychoanalytic theories that had been dismissed by most gay liberationists made its way into radical lesbian politics.

Rich's argument was not "lesbian separatist" in a technical sense, since it rejected the sharp distinctions that separatists made between lesbian and heterosexual women. However, its emphasis on the moral and emotional gulf between all men and all women was in keeping with the practical and philosophical separations that lesbian feminism often encouraged. Gay male sexuality, according to Rich, was typified by anonymous sexual encounters that exalted the pursuit of empty pleasure divorced from feeling. A common stigma was virtually the only tie binding gay men and lesbians.

The late 1970s and early 1980s saw an outpouring of writing and action by lesbians of color who challenged white lesbians' focus on gender to the exclusion of addressing serious divisions among women based on class, race, and culture. Organizations like the Combahee River Collective (a consciousness-raising and political group of African-American women) and Kitchen Table: Women of Color Press (which has published writings by African-American, Latina, and Asian women) were often led by lesbians and emphasized their concerns but did not exclude heterosexual women of color, since these activists saw sexuality as only one of several crucial dimensions of their identity.

In keeping with this insistence on considering an orientation toward other women in holistic perspective, women of color generally stayed away from debates focused exclusively on lesbian sexuality, preferring to frame questions in their own terms. In an influential essay, "The Uses of the Erotic," black poet Audre Lorde defined the erotic as transcending genital sexuality to encompass all aspects of creativity and power. "The erotic is not a question only of what we do; it is a question of how acutely and fully we can feel in the doing. Once we know the extent to which we are capable of feeling that sense of satisfaction and completion, we can then observe which of our various life endeavors bring us closest to that fullness," Lorde wrote.

Lorde's autobiographical *Zami: A New Spelling of My Name* includes lively portraits of black working-class woman-to-woman sexuality that might or might not be openly defined as lesbian, as well as sketches of the white-dominated "gay girl" Greenwich Village scene of the 1950s. Similarly, Chicana poet and playwright Cherríe Moraga insists that lesbian desire be understood not as a timeless essence of woman bonding but in terms of its class- and culture-specific dimensions.

In the 1980s, gay male and lesbian communities drew closer together again, until eventually it became possible to say "lesbian and gay" as though it were one word—at least part of the time. The devastating impact of AIDS on gay men had much to do with this, for as large numbers of lesbians got involved in AIDS work, by joining groups like ACT UP or simply supporting friends who had become ill, they developed tight bonds of solidarity with men they recognized as doing their heroic best to cope with a horrendous burden of fear, physical suffering, and grief. Male communities changed as well, becoming more appreciative of what lesbians had to offer and more willing to listen to feminist criticism. Although important distinctions between the groups had not entirely vanished, it became more likely that theories of same-sex behavior would once again be asked to account for the experiences of both genders.

Increasingly, people of color confronted racism within gay and lesbian organizations, pointing out that their own needs and priorities often remained unmet by agendas that suited the visions of an overwhelmingly white leadership, while their lives were relegated to the sidelines of gay cultural production. Gay men of color took inspiration from lesbians like Lorde and Moraga. As Joseph Beam wrote, explaining the inspiration for the groundbreaking black gay anthology *In the Life*:

> By mid-1983 I had grown weary of reading literature by white gay men who fell, quite easily, into three camps: the incestuous literati of

Manhattan and Fire Island, the San Francisco cropped-moustache-clones, and the Boston-to-Cambridge politically correct radical faggots. None of them spoke to me as a Black gay man....As Black gay men, we have always existed in the African-American community. We have been ministers, hairdressers, entertainers, sales clerks, civil rights activists, teachers, play-wrights, trash collectors, dancers, government officials, choir masters, and dishwashers. You name it; we've done it—most often with scant recognition.

At the same time, a small but vocal bisexual movement had appeared to challenge the prevalent bipolar model of sexual identity. It became increasingly common to see the words "lesbian, gay, and bisexual" in listings of events and names of organizations. The word "queer" was popularized to mean people who espouse a range of unconventional sexual practices, not just exclusive same-sex eroticism. Nevertheless, an in-between status remained especially controversial

Members of the radical gay rights group ACT UP demonstrate for increased AIDS awareness in Paris, France, in 1990. Are gays and lesbians essentially "just like everyone else," except for the matter of sexual orientation, or do they constitute a radically different minority with its own distinct culture? Gays and lesbians themselves disagree on the answer to this question.

among lesbians, as I discovered in 1990 when *OUT/LOOK* magazine published my essay exploring the implications of my relationship with a man. The magazine received a flood of outraged letters to the editor, with a typical viewpoint being, as one reader asserted, that my opposite-sex involvement constituted "failure as a woman-identified woman. The bottom line is: I don't consider any woman a 'dyke' who sleeps with a man."

The late 1980s and early 1990s were a time of escalating political attacks on the precious gains so recently won in the fight for recognition of the rights of sexual minorities. Homophobes mobilized images of gay people as AIDS carriers, and they argued that laws and regulations forbidding discrimination on the basis of sexual orientation actually constitute special protection for homosexuals. Antigay campaigns proved such a potent fund-raiser that political conservatives discovered they could be used to fund a host of other pet causes.

This charged atmosphere set the stage for the current clash between the philosophic heirs of gay liberation and the descendants of the more mainstream 1970s gay movement. Among other things, the disagreement is between those who want to celebrate and amplify differences between themselves and the conventional heterosexual world and those who would opt to downplay those differences—to argue, much as Sergeant Matlovich argued, that they are really just normal Americans whose sexuality pretty much resembles that of the straight majority except for the accident of same-sex orientation. The former group might be referred to as maximizers; the latter, as minimizers.

Today's maximizers tend to favor social constructionist understandings. They often argue historically and comparatively. They like to focus on those interesting places where identity gets shaky rather than hunt for airtight causal explanations. Maximizers can draw on a rapidly growing body of research and theory being produced within academic settings, where constructionism is popular though not unchallenged.

Minimizers are more often essentialist in outlook and more frequently embrace the biological findings that have been so widely publicized. Many minimizers would agree with gay journalist Randy Shilts, who felt that a biological explanation for sexual orientation "would reduce being gay to something like being left-handed." Or they might go further to claim that biological findings show nature's approval of same-sex behavior; such was the implication of a comment by George Neighbors, Jr., a spokesman for the Federation of Parents and Friends of Lesbians and Gays (P-FLAG), who hailed the news of the Hamer gene study with the remark, "If you believe in God or Nature, that's what homosexuality develops from."

Though he wrote in a different context—an exchange among academics on the political implications of using the word "queer"—maximizer Todd Shepard could have been rebutting Neighbors's comments when he declared, "The great queer nightmare should be that 90% of our fellows [will] think of themselves as normal heterosexuals and 10% as normal homosexuals."

Of course, this quick summary is too sketchy and simplistic. Essentialism and constructionism do not always line up so neatly with political positions; the most militant advocates of the activist group Queer Nation's "in your face" tactics have sometimes espoused essentialist notions of queer identity. Essentialism need not rest on biological theories. And often, perhaps even always, conflicting beliefs uneasily coexist within individuals. I myself notice that, despite my rejection of essentialist labels for my own sexual identity, what I often want to know about someone I've just met is precisely, "What *is* she?" or, "Is this guy gay or straight?"

Even the most enthusiastic constructionists have to fudge a little to survive in the real world, according to M. Morgan Holmes, who reports that he identifies as a "queer literature instructor" in the classroom and a "'gay' white male" for weekend activities like cruising, since "whether or not same-sex desire originates in social conditioning, Xq28 [a reference to Hamer's gene study], or a combination of cultural and genetic factors, many people in Western society experience being gay, lesbian, bisexual, or transgendered as essential to selfhood." In other words, it is useful to be queer when you want to suspend certainty in order to pose interesting questions, but when you want to relate to others, it may become strategically necessary to act as though your desires consistently matched up with a recognized identity label.

In 1990, Miguel Gutierrez told an *OUT/LOOK* interviewer of his own set of conflicts over the implications of the queer movement:

> It's still a privileged thing to be queer. I don't feel it's inclusive—there are race and class issues around this. There are people who cannot afford to be nonassimilationist; they are fighting just to eat and live....Then I see *Newsweek*'s article on "Today's Youth," with its token white gay boy who's decided that he's not into promiscuity, wants a husband, kids, a house, and I know that I'm not represented by him, and that I don't identify with his priorities. In that sense, I am queer.

Maximizers and minimizers, social constructionists and essentialists, and those in between—all must reckon with, whether or not they approve of, the enormous impact of scientific findings upon public opinion. Social constructionists, who tend to disapprove, sometimes react with a call to ignore science. More often they respond with questions similar to those they ask on other occasions. They inquire in whose interests appeals to nature function; they investigate the historical roots of current intellectual fashion; they take apart the language in which findings are reported to bare hidden assumptions that extend far beyond surface claims. These tactics contribute valuable insights, but by themselves they are unsatisfactory in that they beg the question of the status of science: does it or doesn't it have any legitimate place in our understanding of forms of desire?

Nonscientists (myself included) tend to react with a curious combination of mistrust and awe to the power of science. Our world has been almost totally reshaped as a result of scientific discoveries, a fact brought to our attention on a daily basis through our use of advanced gadgetry such as computers and cellular phones; our nagging worries about events such as nuclear accidents and global warming that seem to represent science and technology run amok; and our exposure to popularized media accounts of gene mapping, AIDS research, and subatomic physics. Yet most people possess only general and extremely limited scientific knowledge, while an in-depth comprehension of theoretical and technical advances in any scientific field requires intense specialization. A layperson reading a report on, for instance, a claimed link between same-sex behavior and genetic inheritance may feel reduced to a choice between concluding that "scientists say it, so it must be so" or muttering "science is bunk" and walking away from the problem. Either way, she or he remains passive, unable to exercise critical judgment.

In the hope of enabling the reader to avoid this impasse, the next two chapters will take a closer look at recent scientific research into the causes of sexual orientation. We will consider not only the claims of researchers themselves but how these have been received by scientific critics and how they fit into larger trends in biology and genetics.

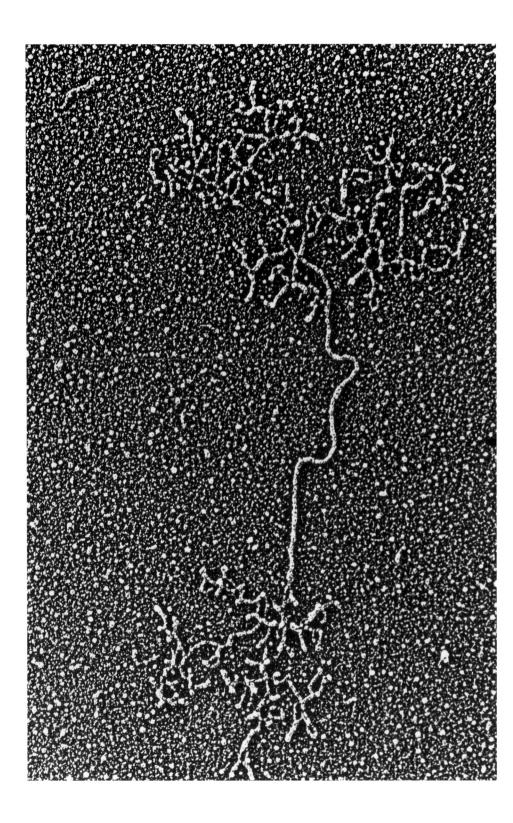

5

The "Science
of Desire"...

IN THE LATE 20TH century, the old scientific fascination with correlations between external physiology and sexual behavior has largely given way to a focus on subtle physical variations that are far more difficult to observe—accessible, if at all, only to powerful microscopes and other advanced technology. That does not mean that the modern era has entirely done away with the belief that sexual difference must be written on the outside of the body; as late as 1948, a physician named R. L. Dickinson published the results of a study comparing the size and other characteristics of the genitals of 31 lesbians with those of heterosexual women he saw in his gynecological practice, while in 1994 a Canadian research team claimed to have discovered differences between the fingerprint whorls of gay and straight men. But for the most part research now focuses on variations at the cellular and subcellular levels.

The long strand at center is a gene, magnified 79,300 times in this electron microscope photograph. Genes encode the information that enables the synthesis of specific proteins, thus specifying the transmission of inherited characteristics.

Almost all of the current scientific studies still treat homosexuality—not heterosexuality or bisexuality—as the phenomenon demanding explanation. Today's scientific investigators, a number of whom are openly gay men, typically describe same-sex attraction as a normal variation rather than an abnormality or perversion, yet their research focus continues to suggest that opposite-sex behavior is the yardstick by which all other behavior is to be judged, the measuring tool that escapes measurement. Since research approaches have been devised with gay men rather than lesbians in mind, a second yardstick is implicit: male homosexuality is to be viewed as the standard for same-sex behavior in general.

In recent years, these approaches have zeroed in on three main areas of inquiry: hormonal influences on the development of sexuality, sex-linked brain dimorphism (that is, polarized differences between particular brain structures in males and females), and genetic factors. Some scientists argue the plausibility of an interrelationship among the three (for instance, a genetic influence on hormones might in turn affect structures in the brain), though as yet such proposals are highly speculative.

Described in general terms, hormones are chemicals that, when secreted into the bloodstream by glandular cells, carry messages to various regions of the body. Diverse sorts of hormones are involved in a vast range of bodily functions. Of special concern to researchers into sexual behavior are the so-called sex hormones, the estrogens and androgens, which were first isolated and synthesized in the 1920s. Despite the fact that estrogens are usually thought of as female and androgens as male, hormones of both types are found in everyone but are present in different proportions and play different roles at different stages in the life of the organism, depending on its sex.

Initially, the embryo is sexually undifferentiated (that is, one that is going to be a male looks the same as a future female). Through the influence of hormones, including testosterone, the genetically male fetus (one with an XY chromosome pair instead of the female XX) develops its male genitalia. Female development is usually described as proceeding automatically in the absence of male hormones, though this notion of "female as lack" has been criticized by some scientists, who call for further investigation.

The sex hormones also play a vital role in the physiology of postnatal sexuality—so that, for instance, a man can be "chemically castrated" by having his hormone balance altered. Reasoning along lines that parallel the early sexological concept of homosexuality as an inversion of normal male or female desire (the "female soul trapped in a male body" idea), researchers suspected that levels of sex hormones in the bodies of adults determined their sexual orientation. Acting on this theory without even bothering to wait for experimental confirmation, some doctors attempted to "cure" male homosexuality with testosterone injections. Especially popular in the 1940s, the theory was ultimately disproved; there are no differences in circulating hormone levels between straight and gay men.

Next, attention turned to the possible effect of prenatal hormone levels on subsequent sexual development. What if hormonal influences somehow wired the fetal brain for same-sex or opposite-sex orientation? This theory is still current, though it has yet to be proved; one of its most ardent proponents, the German endocrinologist Gunther Dörner, ran into a dead end in his efforts at experimental confirmation.

Dörner compared the responses of gay and straight men to injections of estrogens, claiming that the gay men's bodies reacted with a surge of hormones similar to that observed in estrogen-injected female rats. Unfortunately for his theory, the experimental evidence could not be satisfactorily reproduced by other researchers—an essential step in the verification of any experimental finding. Nevertheless, he continued to develop the idea that he had first advanced to explain the supposed estrogen reactions: namely, that a prenatal androgen deficiency could have predisposed gay men's brain circuits to develop in a "female" direction.

Critics have objected to the correlation of rat and human sexual behavior on which this theory depends. They argue that while mating behavior in adult rodents has indeed been shown to be affected by early hormone exposure, it is a long way from a male rat's display of lordosis (bending of the back when mounted, typical of females) to a male human's lovemaking with another man. They also note that Dörner's hypothesis would seem to predict large numbers of homosexuals among men known to have experienced a prenatal androgen deficiency and women exposed to excessive prenatal androgens, but such is not the case.

Dörner clearly saw homosexuality as an undesirable abnormality, so much so that in the 1970s he caused a storm of protest with a proposal that pregnant women have the sex of their fetuses tested and, if found to be carrying males, get testosterone injections to insure that the child would not become gay. Recently his theories have been taken up by a new generation of sex researchers who see themselves as far more positive about sexual variations. Dean Hamer, the principal researcher on a famous "gay gene" study, has invoked hormonal influences as a possible means of explaining how sexual orientation might be biologically determined. Simon LeVay, a gay neuroanatomist who has studied the brains of straight and gay men, explicitly invokes Dörner's idea that "homosexuality, like heterosexuality, results at least in part from specific interactions between androgenic sex hormones and the brain during development."

Published in 1991, LeVay's brain study caused a sensation. He announced that an investigation of the size of certain cell groups, or nuclei, located in a region known as the medial preoptic area of the hypothalamus had produced evidence of a significant dimorphism (structural difference) in gay versus straight men. Although LeVay himself pointed out that such a difference did not necessarily imply a causal connection between brain structure and sexual orientation, much of the media response was far less cautious. *Time* magazine ran a story headlined "Are Gay Men Born That Way?" while *Science,* overlooking the fact that LeVay had not studied lesbians, included both genders, inquiring "Is Homosexuality Biological?"

LeVay's research drew on prior efforts by other investigators to identify sexually dimorphic cell groups in the brains of experimental animals and humans. That is, researchers have sought to identify structural distinctions between male and female brains, thereby hoping to account for what are thought to be gender-typical behaviors.

Like the tradition of inquiry into physiological peculiarities assumed to account for homosexuality, the history of efforts to relate social differences to differences in innate predisposition as determined by brain structure is an unsavory one. It can be traced back to the 19th-century mania for explaining the supposed intellectual inferiority of white women and all African people by measuring brain weight. Gustave Le Bon, an early social psychologist, wrote in 1879:

> In the most intelligent races ... there are a large number of women where brains are closer in size to those of gorillas than to the most developed male brains.... All psychologists who have studied the intelligence of women ... recognize today that they represent the most inferior forms of human evolution and that they are closer to children and savages than to an adult, civilized man.

Some observers fear that the current research into sexual dimorphism in human brains merely represents a refinement of this thinking, and that any positive results will be used to justify an inferior social role for women and those whose brains are judged womanlike. The researchers themselves undoubtedly believe they are simply conducting an objective investigation with the increasingly sophisticated tools at their disposal.

Bearing in mind this chapter's objective—to assess scientific claims by the standards of science—and the fact that "different from" need not mean "worse or better than," we can go on to pose the question: How well does the evidence of dimorphism in the human brain hold up, and to the extent that it does, what if anything does it explain? For reasons the following discussion will clarify, I believe the answer to the first part of the question is "so-so," and to the second, "We don't know."

Located at the base of the brain, the hypothalamus is tiny though important—a "mere teaspoonful of brain tissue" in humans, as LeVay explains it. In 1978, a research team at the University of California at Los Angeles (UCLA), headed by Robert Gorski, identified a nucleus or group of cells in the rat hypothalamus that appeared to be significantly larger in males than in females. The findings were considered especially significant because the hypothalamic region in which he identified the cell group, the medial preoptic area, has been directly associated with mammalian sexual behavior. The cell group itself has been shown to be influenced by hormonal levels around the time of birth, although researchers have never identified a precise function for it.

Working in Gorski's lab, researcher Laura Allen tried to discover whether the human brain contains any comparable dimorphisms. She identified four sets of nuclei, called the first, second, third, and fourth interstitial nuclei of the anterior hypothalamus—INAH1, 2, 3, and 4, for short. INAH2 and 3 were found to be sexually dimorphic, with the male-female difference more pronounced in INAH3.

It should be stressed that, although some believe INAH3 can be considered the human equivalent of the rat's sexually dimorphic nucleus, no one has provided direct evidence that any of the interstitial nuclei are connected to human sexual behavior. Another reason why the results of research on human brain dimorphism are considered inconclusive by some experts has to do with the problem of replicability—that is, whether the results of these extremely delicate tests can be duplicated by other researchers. A group in the Netherlands found sexual dimorphism in INAH1, contrary to Allen's finding; also contradicting her results, Simon LeVay reported no dimorphism in INAH2. It is quite conceivable that future research will cast doubt on the existence of dimorphism in INAH3, the crux of LeVay's research. Writing in *Scientific American,* neuroanatomist and psychiatrist William Byne notes that "human neuroanatomical studies of this kind have a very poor track record for reproducibility."

LeVay performed his study of homosexual-heterosexual dimorphism on tissue samples taken from the brains of 19 men who had died of AIDS and whose hospital charts identified them as homosexual and on similar samples from the brains of 16 men who were presumed heterosexual, six of whom also had died of AIDS. He included a comparison group of brain samples from six women. Medical records were his only source of information as to the sexuality of his subjects. While the charts of those who died of causes other than AIDS failed to specify sexual orientation, he assumed that, based on statistical probability, not more than one or two were likely to have been gay and so felt justified

Brain researcher Simon LeVay's attempt to determine whether there is a biological component to sexual orientation in gay men has generated widespread media attention and scientific criticism.

in using them to represent the "heterosexual" male and female brain.

LeVay set up a coding system so that he would not know which brain sample he was working with at any given time. He then cut each hypothalamus into extremely thin slices, mounted them on slides, and, using a cell-staining technique to aid his observations, examined the tissue under a microscope.

LeVay later summarized his results as follows:

> Like Allen and Gorski, [I] observed that INAH3 was more than twice as large in the [straight] men as in the women. But INAH3 was also between two and three times larger in the straight men than in the gay men. In some gay men...the cell group was altogether absent. Statistical analysis indicated the probability of this result's being attributed to chance was about one in 1,000. In fact, there was no significant difference between volumes of INAH3 in the gay men and in the women. So the investigation suggested a dimorphism related to male sexual orientation about as great as that related to sex.

If confirmed, this correlation between brain structure and sexual orientation could logically be accounted for by supposing that brain makeup determines behavior in a one-way process, but since biologists increasingly recognize the manifold ways in which life experience shapes neuroanatomy, it could just as well be supposed that same-sex behavior influences brain structure. Or both brain structure and behavior could be influenced by some third factor. LeVay admits these alternatives but thinks it more likely that "the structural differences arose during brain development and consequently contributed to sexual behavior."

LeVay's methodology and interpretation have been criticized by several experts in the field. For one thing, there have been questions about whether AIDS—the cause of death for all of the research subjects identified as gay—could have affected the size of INAH3. LeVay thinks this unlikely for several reasons, including the fact that INAH3s in the subjects who died of AIDS and were identified as heterosexual were comparable in size to those of the presumed heterosexuals who did not have AIDS. William Byne argues that, given the small number of apparently heterosexual men with AIDS in the study, there is still a chance that the observed dimorphism might have been caused by AIDS-related hormone abnormalities.

Anne Fausto-Sterling, an expert in developmental genetics who teaches medical science at Brown University, has expressed skepticism about the fact that the range of sizes found for INAH3 almost completely overlaps in the "gay" and "straight" samples. In other words, while on average the men identified as homosexual had smaller versions of this particular nucleus, in some individual cases presumed gays had large INAH3s and presumed straights had small ones.

Both William Byne and feminist anthropologist Carole Vance have pointed to a logical gap between the model of male homosexuality central to LeVay's study and what we know of cross-cultural variations in same-sex behavior. Rather like the notions of the early sexologists, LeVay's model suggests that a gay man is, neurologically speaking, a "feminized" man. However, as we know, a number of cultures regard male-male sexual behavior as perfectly compatible with (or even necessary to) their definitions of masculinity. LeVay's indirect reliance on rat studies for a rationale for his own project raises the question: Does he think that the size of INAH3 is correlated with desire for a male or female sexual partner, or rather with what is assumed to be male-typical behavior such as mounting and penetration? In studies of the effects of early hormone exposure on mating behavior in the adult rat, "normality" in the male was defined by mounting behavior, not the sex of the object of that behavior. But the prevailing North American view defines homosexuality on the basis of sexual object, not sexual act.

Vance and others have been struck by the contrast between the care with which LeVay measured his brain samples and the sloppiness of his assumptions concerning his subjects' sexuality. He had no idea how hospital workers arrived at the conclusion that the AIDS patients for whom they recorded a sexual orientation were indeed gay. Given what is known of human sexual diversity, it seems safe to assume that LeVay's simple labels covered a wide range of specific desires and behaviors. Those subjects who did not die of AIDS were simply assumed, in the absence of evidence to the contrary, to be heterosexual—a peculiarly heterosexist assumption for a gay male researcher to make. In writing up his findings, LeVay also mentioned that in fact one of the subjects had been identified as bisexual but was lumped in with the homosexual sample. This confusion exemplifies a host of problems plaguing LeVay's or any other study that assumes that homosexuality is a single entity or neglects serious investigation of the range of feelings and behaviors that fall outside the hetero-homo dichotomy. Related problems surface in Dean Hamer's gene study.

In general, when scientists perform research on a small number of subjects, as was the case with LeVay, chances increase that a few unusual individuals could skew the results. No matter the size of the sample, universally accepted scientific standards require that the findings be duplicated by other researchers before they can be regarded as firmly established. Even if this eventually happens with LeVay's results, it is unclear what, if anything, the brain dimorphism would indicate about possible causes of sexual orientation.

LeVay himself has been modest in his explicit claims about the implications of his findings, careful to acknowledge that a full account of human sexuality will require examining a mix of biological and environmental factors. Yet in his book *The Sexual Brain,* he waxes broadly optimistic in forecasting discoveries that he is certain will eventually reveal biology in the driver's seat: "Given the explosive rate at which the fields of molecular genetics and neurobiology are expanding, it is inevitable that the perception of our own nature, in the field of sex as in all attributes of our physical and mental lives, will be increasingly dominated by concepts derived from the biological sciences." In interviews he has been frank about his sense that biological determinism offers the best explanation of his own experience and that of other gay men: "Basically I tend to sympathize with people who say this [i.e. his brain research] proves what I have always thought—that I was born that way. That it wasn't thought processes or interpersonal relationships later in life."

Feeling with LeVay that biology holds the key, if not to all the secrets of human sexuality then at least to the most important ones, researchers have recently been looking at evidence for a genetic influence on homosexuality. The existence of a gay gene was postulated by Edward O. Wilson, originator of the influential and controversial application of genetics known as sociobiology, in 1975. Since the mid-1980s, Richard Pillard, an openly gay professor of psychiatry who played an important role in the American Psychiatric Association's 1973 decision to stop classifying homosexuality as a psychological disorder, has been hot on the trail of evidence that homosexuality runs in families. Like LeVay, he hopes that his research will have beneficial consequences for the gay community.

Together with Michael Bailey, a psychologist, Pillard has investigated genetic input into both male and female same-sex orientation. For their study of males, the two recruited gay men who had either a twin brother or an adopted brother. They then compared the incidence of homosexuality in the twin and adoptive siblings. In each case, sexual orientation was established by means of interview questions probing for what was meant by the self-applied labels (for instance, whether a self-description as gay might include significant bisexual experience). They found that about half of the gay men who were identical (monozygotic) twins had gay or "substantially bisexual" twin brothers. For the fraternal (dizygotic) twin pairs, the match was about 20 percent, while for the adoptive pairs it was about 11 percent.

Running their data through a computer program designed to eliminate glitches such as possible bias in the recruitment of their subjects, they confirmed the conclusion suggested by the raw percentages: given that identical twins share an identical genetic makeup, fraternal twins share half of their genes, and adoptive brother pairs share none, the much stronger pairing of gay identical twins points to a significant genetic factor influencing sexual orientation. (If, for instance, home environment was the only factor influencing homosexuality, one would expect to find the same number of gay brother pairs in the adoptive set as in the identical and fraternal twins.)

Bailey and Pillard later did a similar study on lesbians and their siblings and came up with results very close to those for the men, suggesting a substantial genetic factor for female homosexuality as well. However, Pillard later confessed to an interviewer his doubts that female sexuality can be properly understood using the same sorts of measures devised for the male study:

> I think women are much more flexible in their sexual orientation—they don't as often label themselves as gay or straight. Usually when you ask that question of men, at least men over the age of thirty or thirty-five, a few will say they're bisexual but most will say they're gay or straight; they dichotomize. Women often will say, "Well, it depends on whom I'm with, on what sort of relationship I'm having..." And they'll often have had relationships that are lesbian and relationships that are heterosexual. They're quite functional and quite involved in both those kinds of relationships. You might want to call more women bisexual, which we end up doing, but I think women's orientation is really much more complicated than men's sexual orientation. I think it's really a harder thing to study in the quantitative way that we've been doing.

This comment vividly illustrates the perils of investigating women's

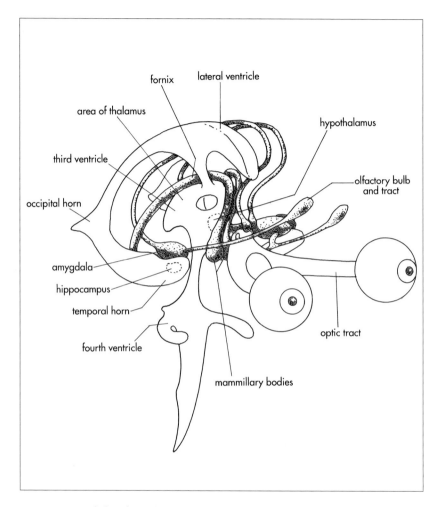

LeVay's research has focused on apparent differences in the hypothalamus section of the brain in gay men as a possible key to a biological explanation for sexual desire. The hypothalamus helps regulate several important bodily functions, including body temperature, blood pressure, heartbeat, and blood sugar level.

sexuality using models devised for men (which, by the way, LeVay hopes to do with further research on brain structure and orientation). As Bailey and Pillard did in classifying women as bisexual despite the suspicion that the label was inadequate to describe a complex reality, inves–

tigators may be tempted to manipulate their findings to fit the male model, thus avoiding the need to describe and explain important differences that may exist between the two genders. The Bailey and Pillard research also discounts the possibility of significant differences in sexuality based on race and class, since their subjects have been almost entirely white and more economically privileged than the general population.

Pillard emphasizes that he looks to an interaction of environmental and genetic factors to explain why people become gay, yet, like LeVay, he often seems to place more weight on the heritable (genetic) portion of the equation than on the environmental side. In an Op-Ed piece on their research published in the *New York Times* in December 1991, Bailey and Pillard asserted that "science is rapidly converging on the conclusion that sexual orientation is innate," adding that this is "good news for homosexuals and their advocates" because it will debunk the homophobic notion that older gays "recruit" young people.

Dean Hamer's genetic study, the results of which were published in 1993, has been judged an impressive piece of research even by professionals who are generally skeptical of biological explanations for human sexuality. Building on the results of the Bailey and Pillard study of males, Hamer and his colleagues first examined the incidence of gay male relatives within families but then went a step further, actually looking at genetic material—DNA—from pairs of gay brothers. They found that the pairs shared a particular region of the X chromosome, called Xq28, at a rate significantly higher than would be predicted by chance, leading to the conclusion that a gene located on the X chromosome plays some role in the sexual orientation of between five and 30 percent of gay men.

In view of the complexity of Hamer's research and the misleading nature of much media coverage, it is important to stress that Hamer did not discover an actual gene—only the general area of the X chromosome within which the gene is presumed to be located. Even if such a gene is discovered, it can help to account for only a small percentage of male homosexuality; by no means everyone who is homosexual would have the gene, and simply possessing the gene would not be enough, in and of itself, to cause a homosexual orientation. Hamer did not study the Xq28 region in pairs of gay and straight brothers, but he presumes that some straight brothers of gay men would share the hypothetical gene. He cautions that even when much more is known about genes, it will be impossible to make accurate predictions about people's sexuality based on genetic analysis "because of the complex interplay of the genes with many different biological, environmental, social, cultural, and temporal factors."

These are crucial qualifications because a major attraction of biological explanations of sexuality lies in their seeming ability to account for individual sexuality in a way that social constructionist theories fail to do. Reports of a gay gene arouse the expectation that the question, "Why did Sergeant Matlovich (or James Baldwin, or Larry Kramer) grow up to be attracted to men instead of women?" will receive a clear, conclusive answer. Yet, as Hamer puts it, "Our results were based purely on statistical measurements of a group and can say nothing about individual people."

Like Simon LeVay and Richard Pillard, Hamer tends to waver between limited claims for the implications of his own research and optimistic claims for the powerful role he believes biology can play in our future understanding of sexuality. The title of his book, *The Science of Desire: The Search for the Gay Gene and the Biology of Behavior,* seems to suggest that science really has succeeded in explaining desire and that a single gay gene definitely exists and is likely to be found soon. Both because of the intrinsic interest of Hamer's finding that five to 30 percent of male homosexuality is genetically linked—that is, influenced by inheritance—and because of the immense popular appeal of little-understood genetic theories, it is well worth taking a closer look at his research method and conclusions.

First, a bit of background on genes and chromosomes. In everyday speech, we tend to speak of genes as though they were things, self-contained and observable—like beads on a string, or peas in a pod. The language in which the news media report scientific findings often reinforces this view, proclaiming that a gene for this or that has been identified. The layperson may imagine a scientist peering through a microscope and muttering "Eureka!" as the gene swims into view. To biologists, however, genes are not objects but fragments of information, pieces of DNA molecules that specify the sequences of amino acids that will make up a particular protein (a crucial substance within all living organisms) or influence how and when the protein will be synthesized.

Within each cell of the human body are 23 chromosome pairs, each made up of one chromosome contributed by the mother and one from the father. Each chromosome contains a single long DNA molecule with instructions for making vast numbers of proteins. The specific, minuscule segment of the Xq28 region of the X chromosome in which Dean Hamer hypothesizes his gay gene is located has room for about 200 genes.

Hamer's focus on the X chromosome in his search for a genetic link to male homosexuality resulted from his observation that the gay men in families in his sample were not evenly spread throughout the family tree but appeared to be clustered in identifiable patterns. Fourteen percent of men with gay brothers were themselves gay, as opposed to two percent of men without gay brothers. (Hamer is aware that this last statistic falls very much on the low end of estimates of the occurrence of male homosexuality in the general population. He used what he terms a "stringent definition" of orientation—classifying as "definitely homosexual" only those who openly identified as such.)

Besides the relatively high incidence of gay brothers, Hamer also noticed a pattern of homosexuality in male relatives of the mothers of gay men—but not male relatives of those men's fathers. This suggested to him that any genetic component must be passed down through the mothers.

Since the 22 autosomal (nonsex) chromosomes contain DNA segments contributed by either father or mother, and his evidence indicated an inheritance only through the mother, Hamer speculated that male homosexuality could be linked to a gene on the X chromosome, the half of the XY pair of sex chromosomes that a man receives from his mother. (Women get two Xs, one from each parent.) He then recruited pairs of gay brothers, obtained DNA samples from them, and analyzed their X chromosomes. He was looking for what are known as DNA markers, segments of DNA that indicate specific locations on the chromosome and, while their functions may differ completely from that of the gene being searched for, nevertheless point to the proximity of genes that tend to be inherited together.

At each marker, he checked to see whether the brother pairs were concordant (that is, whether their markers were identical); since siblings share 50 percent of their genetic material, chance would dictate that half of the markers would match up. He describes the outcome:

> The results of this study were striking. Over most of the X chromosome the markers were randomly distributed between the gay brothers. But at the tip of the long arm of the X chromosome, in a region known as Xq28, there was a considerable excess of concordant [matched] brothers: 33 pairs shared the same marker, whereas only seven pairs did not. Although the sample size was not large, the result was statistically significant: the probability of such a skewed ratio occurring by chance alone is less than one in 200. In a control group of 314 randomly selected pairs of brothers, most of whom can be presumed to be heterosexual, Xq28 markers were randomly distributed.

To put this in perspective, it is important to note that the markers were identical only within given brother pairs, not from pair to pair. A marker is not a gene; it is only a piece of DNA that points to the existence of a gene in its vicinity. From the evidence of shared markers, Hamer can plausibly claim a genetic influence on some instances of same-sex orientation in males, even though a gene has not been identified.

Like LeVay's brain study, Hamer's research still needs to be replicated. As is true for all complex studies, its design and conclusions are open to challenge on a variety of levels; for instance, statistics expert Neil J. Risch has questioned its statistical significance, and William Byne and others feel that Hamer should have done a comparative study on the Xq28 region of gay-straight brother pairs.

Although he used a fairly detailed questionnaire to determine his subjects' orientation, Hamer seems almost as naive as LeVay in his failure to question sexual categories. He believes almost everybody can be reliably identified as either gay or straight. It never occurs to him that this finding in his self-selected sample of overwhelmingly white, well-to-do, politically liberal, "out" gay men and their families might not hold true for other populations. If he had considered bisexuals to be of any importance, he might have been more puzzled by the fact that his proposed gay gene seems unable to explain an intermediate or mixed orientation.

Nevertheless, in combination with Bailey and Pillard's twin studies, Hamer's work provides the most suggestive evidence to date that sexual orientation has a partial basis in biological "givens," at least in some male individuals. (While Hamer believes that twin and family studies provide strong evidence for genetic factors in lesbianism, his own work has not turned up any specific patterns of inheritance that could help suggest which portions of which chromosomes might be involved.)

All accounts of the possible workings of a genetic influence—understood to interact in unpredictable fashion with untold numbers of nongenetic factors, ranging from the intrauterine environment to the psychological and cultural surroundings—are at this point highly speculative. During the course of his research Hamer tested and rejected several hypotheses having to do with hormone mechanisms. He remains intrigued by the possibility that a gene on the X chromosome might play a role in the variations in brain structure investigated by Simon LeVay.

While Hamer's hypotheses assume that a genetically influenced biological mechanism directly affects sexual desire, several other investigators have proposed that genes might operate in a much more indirect fashion to help establish orientation. Ed Stein, who has written on the essentialist-social constructionist controversy and is attempting to find common ground between the two approaches, suggests that genes might affect mental mechanisms—specific dispositions or ways of looking at the world—that, for instance, may predispose modern Americans to identify as gay, whereas in traditional Native American cultures they might have become berdaches.

Neuroscientist William Byne similarly advocates a more complex model: "Particular genes might influence personality traits that could in turn influence the relationships and subjective experiences that contribute to the social learning of sexual orientation." Such proposals, while fully as speculative as Hamer's, at least confront the enormous complexity of types of interactions between genes and environment that reductionists like LeVay and Hamer ritually invoke while giving their real allegiance to more easily measured factors like brain cell clusters and hormone levels. Reductionist thinking will have a difficult time bridg-

Any causal explanation of sexual desire needs to take into account the various manifestations of opposite-sex desire as well as same-sex desire.

ing the huge gap that separates the function of DNA segments known as genes in controlling protein synthesis from the world of meanings embodied in sexual desire for someone of a particular gender.

In other words, it is quite possible to envision a role for genetics and other biological factors in encouraging same-sex or opposite-sex desire while rejecting the determinist explanations supplied by researchers like Hamer, LeVay, and Pillard, who seek to award biology the predominant role in establishing sexual identity. To a large extent, it is a question of

emphasis. William Byne urges us to pay more attention to what the genetic studies indicate about the role of environment:

> Perhaps the major finding of these heritability studies is that despite having all of their genes in common and having prenatal and postnatal environments as close to identical as possible, approximately half of the identical twins were nonetheless discordant for orientation [that is, one twin was gay and one straight]. This finding underscores just how little is known about the origins of sexual orienation.

Observations of the interaction between genetic and environmental factors have shown that in relatively simple organisms, a single genotype (the organism's genetic makeup) can give rise to a wide range of phenotypes (observable characteristics) based on variations in environment. For instance, several cuttings from a single plant may grow and flower quite differently if planted in similar soil at different altitudes. The variations are unpredictable—one plant may grow tall at low and high elevations and short at an intermediate elevation. Since human beings are quite a bit more complex than plants—as are their environments—one can imagine the difficulty of analyzing the pathway from genotype to phenotype in the case of a hypothetical gay gene.

Given all this, what does the recent research really indicate? If one believes that the findings can stand up to the various criticisms that have been leveled at them and will eventually be replicated (probably more likely for the genetic studies than for LeVay's brain research), one is left with evidence that biological factors have something (but not everything) to do with at least some instances of male homosexuality. However, this knowledge has no value in helping to predict or explain the orientation of particular individuals. While it suggests that human beings may not start their lives as entirely blank slates, it says next to nothing about the process whereby whatever is written on the slate to begin with turns into the complex phenomenon we call sexuality. It does not, in other words, provide a causal explanation. It does furnish intriguing hints that feelings and behaviors we tend to lump together as though they must represent a unitary orientation derived from a common cause might in fact represent the outcome of multiple and diverse processes.

So why all the hoopla? Why all the headlines? Why do so many of the scientists behave as though identifying a biological "component" has suddenly unlocked the deepest mysteries of desire? Answering these questions requires going beyond the specific research results to investigate the authority science wields in our culture and the current vogue enjoyed by biological approaches to explaining human social arrangements.

6

...And the Desire for Science

The culture looks for causes. . . . It would be so easy if it [the explanation for sexual orientation] was biology—I could see it being really attractive to people who don't want to have prejudices. . . . Science is our God, so if Science said it was okay, it would be like God said it's okay.

—Jane Hohenberger, college student

The tendency of advertising to promote a certain standard of physical appearance, and thereby to shape popular notions of what is sexually attractive, has become so commonplace as to practically avoid scrutiny.

AS THE PRECEDING DISCUSSION has shown, biological explanations of homosexuality have a long history during which they have waxed and waned in popularity, often recycling familiar themes such as the notion that gay men have feminized bodies. In this sense, the current popularity of biological answers to the causal question represents a continuity with the past. At the same time, the present is unique and must be understood on its own terms. The contemporary mood has been nurtured at the intellectual level by a highly speculative revision of Darwinian thinking called sociobiology, and at the level of funding and publicity by the glamour of an ambitious DNA mapping program, the human genome project. At the political level, it is fed by a craving for theories that would allow a space for sexual difference while excusing us from the daunting but necessary task of rethinking basic values and remolding institutions to combat the injustices resulting from bias based on gender, race, and sexuality.

This does not mean that all claims of discoveries about relationships between biology and sexuality are necessarily false or that most scientists presently engaged in this sort of research do so out of ill will or conscious prejudice. What I am saying is that we need to scrutinize biological explanations very carefully, both to see how well the experimental evidence and interpretations hold up and to gauge the effects of the political and social reasoning that inevitably flows from such claims.

Harvard biologist Edward O. Wilson gave a major boost to genetic determinism with the 1975 publication of his enormously influential *Sociobiology: A New Synthesis.* Wilson's was an ambitious attempt to meld evolutionary theory, genetics, and the social sciences in order to expose what he believed to be the biological underpinnings of social behavior. Sociobiology is an indirect descendant of Darwin's theory of sexual selection—that is, the aspect of species evolution that has to do not with individual fitness for survival but rather with reproductive behavior, which is seen as critical because it affects the chances that an individual's genes will be passed on to succeeding generations. Sociobiologist Richard Dawkins, in his book *The Selfish Gene*, turned this principle into the notion that genes can be viewed as replicator units whose sole purpose is to insure the presence of copies of themselves in succeeding generations.

The theory has been challenged on a multitude of grounds. Some have complained that sociobiological genes correspond suspiciously to the ideal inhabitants of individualist, capitalist society and that sociobiology can claim to explain just about any social phenomenon without deigning to offer proof, since we have such scanty knowledge of evolutionary histories of actual genes. Sociobiology also presents some troubling political implications, insofar as it seems to ratify social phenomena like sexism and violence with its suggestion that these must endure

Edward O. Wilson is perhaps the best-known exponent of sociobiology, which seeks to explain virtually every aspect of human behavior in terms of its evolutionary advantage.

because they have worked to favor gene selection.

As one might guess from this synopsis, sexual behavior looms large in the theory, so it is no surprise to discover that Dean Hamer leans heavily on sociobiological principles, with ready references to "selfish genes" and attempts to explain how a gay gene could exist given its assumed tendency to interfere with reproduction. No wonder Wilson himself endorsed Hamer's *The Science of Desire*, providing a glowing blurb for the back cover.

Hamer considers his main achievement to consist in having offered what he calls the first proof of sociobiology's central tenet—that genes are linked to complex behaviors. He does not mention that claims of genetic links to such complex behaviors as criminality, alcoholism, and manic depression have been widely publicized in recent years, only to be withdrawn when the findings could not be replicated.

Critics of genetic explanations warn that so-called behavioral traits are very different from simple inherited characteristics like eye color, and that to assume that both can be explained by genes in analogous fashion is, in effect, to confuse apples with oranges. As Gisela Kaplan and Lesley Rogers point out in an anthology entitled *Challenging Racism and Sexism: Alternatives to Genetic Explanations*:

> Behavior is at an entirely different level of organization than the genes; many steps and functions separate the two. Genes are expressed as biochemical processes; behavior is expressed by the whole organism. This is not to say that genes play no part in behavior. Rather, it is not possible to ignore the processes of development, to ignore environmental influences on the expression of genes, and to extrapolate directly from genes to behavior as do the sociobiologists.

Hamer's arguments exemplify the fearless but somewhat foolhardy leaps from DNA to behavior that have inspired geneticist Val Woodward to speak of the sociobiological "gene as metaphor." For instance, Hamer writes,

> Perhaps the most important question to ask is not "How could a 'gay gene' evolve?" but "Are there genes for sexuality in general?" Everything we know about evolution and natural selection says there must be. Since evolution selects genes that allow people to reproduce, there must be genes that encourage men and women to have sex and raise children.

Note how this passage confuses "sexuality in general," heterosexual behavior, reproductive sex acts, and the rearing of children. Hamer's effort to generalize from genes to behavior would be immensely complicated by a confrontation with the actual complexities of human psychology, social organization, and cultural forms. Starting from a presupposition that sexuality is an either-or matter and that gay and straight are essential, timeless orientations—his decision to exclude bisexuals from his study was, he says, intentional—Hamer sets up his research in such a way as to bypass any information to the contrary and then comes up with evidence for a gene that in turn seems to confirm his initial categories. Under the sort of scientific-technical approach favored by a Hamer or LeVay, information that does not fit existing theories and preferred modes of research in effect falls into limbo; it is made to disappear, as though it had never existed.

The advances in genetic technology that supported Hamer's research are courtesy of the human genome project, a costly government-funded crash program to identify a base sequence for the DNA in all 23 human chromosomes. The first step in the process is the identification of markers associated with specific traits. Eventually, workers plan to compile a sequence of nucleotide bases—the links within a DNA chain. To give an idea of the complexity of this project, Hamer estimates that the specific region of Xq28 within which he thinks a gay gene is probably located contains five million base pairs; the entire human genome that is eventually to be mapped contains an estimated three billion base pairs.

The compilation of a complete base sequence has been touted by molecular biologists and other advocates as the forerunner of a solution to a variety of social ills or even as offering ultimate insight into what it means to be human. Feminist biologist Ruth Hubbard cautions, however, that because so little is known about just how genetic coding for protein synthesis ultimately affects and is affected by the total functioning of an organism and its interactions with surroundings, there may be little to gain and much to lose from the human genome project. "Though it may not explain what genes 'do,' it will magnify the mythic importance our culture assigns to genes and heredity," Hubbard writes.

The intense media and popular interest in Hamer's limited and questionable results exemplifies that modern mythmaking process. The negative potential of such myths is starkly exemplified by the respectful attention recently given to Richard Herrnstein and Charles Murray's *The Bell Curve,* with its racist and scientifically bankrupt arguments that people of color and poor people are genetically inferior to the white middle class. While Hamer is certainly no Herrnstein or Murray—in fact, he seems very genuinely concerned to counter any threat that his research results could be used to harm gays—his work needs to be seen as part of the same larger trend. Not coincidentally, his book was reviewed in the *New York Times Book Review* along with *The Bell Curve* and the memoirs of Edward O. Wilson, under the headline "How Much of Us Is in the Genes?"

The mythic importance of genes derives largely from the fact that in their metaphoric form, to use Woodward's phrase, they furnish such handy causal explanations of phenomena for which single, obvious causes cannot plausibly be claimed. Feminist geneticist Anne Fausto-Sterling offers her objection to this oversimplified approach: "Despite my general acceptance of Western scientific thought, I find the available concepts and tools of modern science inadequate to describe certain kinds of reality, especially those that are multiply determined—that is, those for which a particular end may be reached by a number of alternate pathways. Complex social behavior is one example."

It is no accident that some of the foremost critics of genetic explanations have been feminists and antiracism activists, since hereditarian reasoning so often runs counter to the interests of women and people of color; Fausto-Sterling's book, for example, is called *Myths of Gender*. The work of these thinkers is highly relevant to the concerns of this chapter, since unexamined gender assumptions underlie biological theories about sexual orientation.

The feminist distinction between gender and sex originated in an effort to challenge essentialist ideas about what it is to be a man or a woman; that is, to question notions of an innate, timeless destiny for people with particular genitals or sets of chromosomes. This challenge was directly connected to the ideology of the early gay liberation movement and of those lesbian feminists who thought that "any woman can be a lesbian." Such people may have been mistaken in some of their convictions about the origins of sexual desire and the plasticity of personal identity, but I believe they were right to resist the assumption that women and men are such inherently and eternally dissimilar creatures that nature could somehow biologically program people for attraction to one and only one sex.

To accept the notion that orientation to same or opposite sex is biologically determined is to do more than decide that homosexuality and heterosexuality are real categories. It is also to bow to the concept that gender is real in some sense that transcends differences between genitals or chromosomes. It is to decide that the meanings we attach to gender (or through which we "make" gender) are somehow not meanings at all but fixed attributes.

But this cannot be the case, since cross-cultural comparisons show that while gender is important everywhere, the specific content of what it means to be male or female varies enormously from culture to culture and even from social class to social class. Think, for instance, of the distance between the Sambia adolescent male, for whom mouth-penis contact is an indispensable element of masculinity, and the "all-American" male, for whom the term "cocksucker" is the worst of insults. Or think of Sojourner Truth, the African-American antislavery leader who in 1851 challenged white society's image of fragile, protected womanhood with her famous "Ain't I a Woman?" speech: "That man over there says that women need to be helped into carriages and lifted over ditches and to have the best place everywhere. Nobody ever helps me into carriages or over mud puddles or gives me the best place. And ain't I a woman?"

What then is desired in a woman or a man? Clearly, something that is drenched in culturally specific meanings, meanings we have both absorbed and helped to create, perhaps particularly in our early years. For certain people, especially both straight and gay men, specific physical traits take on great importance. In one culture or one century, heterosexual males regard fat women as luscious objects of desire; in another, thin is in. Social attributes can also be crucial. In ancient Greece, male citizens eroticized other males who were their social inferiors. The same has been true of British upper-class gay men, as the novels of E. M. Forster and Alan Hollinghurst attest. In the United States today, a quick glance at the personal ads will provide ample evidence that desire for a man or a woman is not a yen for any old torso with penis or vagina attached but rather desire for a clustered set of characteristics that spell

The view that sexual orientation is biologically ordained ignores the existence of countless cultural variations on what it means to be male or female. Anti-slavery leader Sojourner Truth, for example, challenged 19th-century America's notions of womanhood in her famous "Ain't I A Woman?" speech.

"sexually attractive man or woman" to a specific individual.

Or at any rate, this is how I think. I live by gender codes as much as anybody else, but in my heart I don't believe that gender is real in any but a social sense. How could it be, when it so often switches on me? The experience is that of an optical illusion. I'll be walking down a subway platform and I'll think, "That looks like an attractive woman." And I'll walk a few more yards and see that she's a man.

Of course it's possible that I "misread" gender in this way because of some intrauterine testosterone surge that endowed me with an intersexed brain, thus predisposing me to bisexuality. But I don't believe that. I think it's because I've practiced seeing the arbitrariness of gender in communities of lesbians and gay men where playing with the possibilities is part of the culture of desire. I sometimes wear a button with a quote from Patti Smith: "As Far As I'm Concerned, Being Any Gender

Is A Drag." I cherish the words of a student named Tehea, a bisexual woman who wrote, "I'm not attracted to macho men I just like people who redefine their own gender. Yes I think that's exciting."

People who favor biological understandings of sexuality generally do not believe in the possibility of redefining gender; instead, they believe that gender is an innate endowment and that some homing device in the brain or the gonads has the ability to detect gender "oppositeness" or "sameness" and channel us toward it. Hamer, for instance, writes, "In most respects, gay men still are 'real men' and lesbians still are 'real women'" without feeling the need to pause and inquire what "real men and women" are.

Sexologist John Money opines that since sexual orientation determines attraction only to outward body form, "It is not necessary for the body sex of the partner to be in agreement with the chromosomal sex, the gonadal sex (testicles or ovaries), or the sex of the internal reproductive anatomy. For example, a male-to-female, sex-reassigned transsexual with the body morphology [form] transformed to be female in appearance is responded to as a woman." But would just any man who had undergone sex-reassignment surgery be "responded to as a woman?" Does not successful sex reassignment require that one take on the conventional movements and mannerisms, the habits of mind and ways of speech, of the other sex—not *just* its body morphology?

Such considerations bear out the truth of Simone de Beauvoir's aphorism that one is not born but becomes a woman (or, one might add, a man). The gendering process establishes an opposition that is far from natural. As lesbian anthropologist Gayle Rubin put it in her classic essay "The Traffic in Women":

> Men and women are, of course, different. But they are not as different as day and night, earth and sky, yin and yang, life and death. In fact, from the standpoint of nature, men and women are closer to each other than either is to anything else—for instance, mountains, kangaroos, or coconut palms. The idea that men and women are more different from one another than either is from anything else must come from somewhere other than nature.... Far from being an expression of natural differences, exclusive gender identity is the suppression of natural similarities.

Rubin's formulation critiques an understanding of gender as absolute opposition that some observers feel is peculiarly characteristic of Western thought. Will Roscoe, who researched the berdache role among the Zuni, feels that an elastic, nonessentialist concept of gender identity—a notion that gender is acquired rather than given—has fostered the creation of an intermediate gender status among these tribal people. Serena Nanda likewise thinks that the hijras of India, biological males or hermaphrodites who adopt female clothing and a special social role and may undergo surgical castration, are able to occupy a position as "neither man nor woman" because the Hindu worldview encourages the commingling of apparent opposites.

The research of Martin Weinberg, Colin Williams, and Douglas Pryor on a bisexual community in San Francisco in the 1980s, described in their 1994 book *Dual Attraction: Understanding Bisexuality,* provides one example of recent theorizing about sexual orientation that attempts to account for a spectrum of sexual variations. The authors point out that explanations involving brain structures or genes present a problem for the understanding of bisexuality not only because it is hard to see how the proposed mechanisms could predispose someone to both same- and opposite-sex attraction—should we expect to find a bisexual as well as a gay or lesbian gene?—but because biology is ill-equipped to account for the radical changes in sexual desire that some people experience:

> People do not always have an exclusive preference for their own or the opposite sex. Sometimes they are attracted to their own and the opposite sex during the same period in time. Or they may live many years attracted to the opposite sex, but then change their interests to the same sex. Or they may dart around between opposite and same-sex partners with no discernible pattern. These "bisexual" patterns of sexuality are not uncommon.

Weinberg and his colleagues use the term "sexual preference" rather than "orientation" to "emphasize that people take an active part in constructing their sexuality. . . . By this we do not mean that people have complete freedom of choice or that they suddenly decide to be one way or another. But sexual attraction is far more complex than biology allows."

Dual Attraction emphasizes that bisexuality is a difficult identity to maintain because of the societal expectation that people will be either gay or straight. Many bisexuals reported experiencing homophobia from straights while at the same time encountering the attitude among some gay men or lesbians that they were just confused, were avoiding recognition of their "true" homosexual identity, or were taking advantage of heterosexual privilege by failing to come out all the way. The authors did a comparison study of people who defined themselves as homosexual and as heterosexual, from which they concluded that the boundaries between categories are far from absolute; some people who identify as bisexual exhibit desires and behaviors quite similar to those of some people who identify as straight or gay. This raises the possibility that "for persons dealing with the confusions that dual attractions can bring, a sexual identity can *stabilize* sexual preference. If you know what you *are,* it organizes what you *do.*"

The authors found that for heterosexuals and homosexuals alike, early sexual attractions and experiences most often predicted future identity. Frequently those who later came to identify as bisexual had opposite-sex experiences first and added on same-sex behavior at a later date. At the same time, many people of all three sexual identities showed "evidence of a bisexual potential in that their early experiences involved a mix of sexual feelings and behaviors toward both sexes (and this persisted into adulthood for many of them)."

To explain these findings, the authors developed a social learning model of sexual identity that understands what they call preference as flowing from the ways in which people learn where erotic interest is to be directed. In this model, the pleasure that derives from bodily stimulation is given meaning through its association with gender. Everyone learns what is erotic about both genders; to become oriented in an exclusive direction "requires unlearning, disattending to, or repressing desirable features" of either one's own gender (in the case of heterosexuality) or the opposite gender (in the case of homosexuality). Bisexuals possess an "open gender schema" that disconnects the individual's own gender from sexual desire and makes it possible to act on early lessons about the desirability of both men and women.

The researchers were unable to develop a satisfactory theory about precisely how or why particular people end up with an open gender schema. They did note that conscious awareness about gender seemed to play a role for some people. For instance, among bisexual transsexuals they studied, the contradictions and confusions of traditional gender arrangements had been a lifelong theme, resulting in a great deal of thought about how gender and sexuality connect. Many women reported that feminism had helped them to realize that their gender identity was not synonymous with heterosexuality.

Dual Attraction leaves a good deal unexplained. Not only is the theory of the open gender schema unable to suggest why specific people maintain their capacity to attend to what is erotic about both genders, but, most glaringly, it seems unable to account for why gay men and lesbians would "unlearn, disattend to, or repress" opposite-sex attractions when there is so much social pressure to do just the reverse.

Despite these limitations, the study at least attempts to explain sexual identity based on detailed attention to the ways in which people themselves describe and account for their behavior. And it recognizes and affirms a genuine spectrum of variations, rather than excluding some people out of the fear that they will introduce too much inconvenient complexity into the picture. The bisexuality that is profiled in the book is clearly the product of a very particular time and place. The community that the researchers found in the early 1980s had been drastically altered by the devastating impact of AIDS at the end of the decade. What their work suggests, then, is not the discovery of yet another timeless sexual identity, one located exactly halfway between the poles of gay and straight; rather, it suggests the relative power people have to shape their own sexual destinies—not as a matter of convenience or caprice but through an intentional relationship to exquisitely complex patterns of gendered meanings.

A conversation I had with a gay student suggests some of this complexity. Wilber Valenzuela, who grew up in Peru, knew from a very early age that he was different—attracted to men. He wanted to play with dolls, but that was forbidden. His mother sent him to a military school to make him into a proper boy; he suffered a great deal. After moving to the U.S., he was taunted by classmates in a conventional high school. He ended up at Harvey Milk High School, a New York public high school for lesbian and gay youth.

To the 17th-century Flemish painter Peter Paul Rubens and his contemporary audience, these languorous, fleshy women were the epitome of female beauty. But by the cultural standards promulgated by the mass media today, they would probably be regarded as unattractively heavy.

When I met Wilber during his freshman year of college, he was what I would have called a gay nationalist—proud of his identity, totally sure of what it meant, and convinced that everyone else ought to be equally unconflicted. A year later, his perspective was somewhat different. He was still very definitely gay, as I imagine he'll always be, but now he was more interested in the nuances of sexual attraction. He told me that he'd begun experiencing an occasional interest in women, but was stopped from acting on it by being unsure what to do with a female partner. He said he'd heard similar things from gay male friends his age.

I thought: but of course! The prevalent view is that a real man must be able to take the lead in a sexual encounter with a woman—a transaction that requires him to get an erection right away and maintain it to orgasm through vaginal intercourse. It makes perfect sense that gay men who may experience occasional attraction to women would rather avoid this test (which frequently intimidates straight men as well). And that fact, in turn, makes it easy for the passing researcher to conclude that sexual orientation is a cut-and-dried matter.

Tehea, whose comment about people redefining their own genders I quoted previously, reflected in writing on her sometimes contradictory feelings:

> Bisexuals are funny creatures—whether they're trying to be straight or trying to be strictly queer, none of them want to call themselves bisexual. Not even me. Least of all me. I'm bISExual. Mumble cringe cringe. I used to think that once I got over this boy I was in love with for a few years I could not fuck or love boys anymore only girls and I could be good and not ashamed of anything like one of the more Advanced Lesbians....Why do I tense up when my queer girl friends tell me that they're with a man? I see the same ones do it back to me. Are we all reacting out of the same fear that when a person with a penis comes we'll all lose our queerdom like a smell that wears off? A faint whiff.

Her confession sharply evokes the political as well as personal stakes in these debates. Same-sex attraction in the West has been belittled for so long—cast so far into the shadows, so deprived of social space and of all the public, institutional trappings that lend weight and substance to opposite-sex desire—that often the only appropriate response seems to be to adopt what has been called an ethnic model of gay advocacy. This model argues that gays and lesbians are a different sort of people from heterosexuals—different, but comparable: a minority group with a firm identity marked by well-defined boundaries, deserving of rights on that basis.

To point to the blurriness of those boundaries, and the ambiguity of that identity, seems to carry with it the threat that same-sex desire will again be swallowed up, made to disappear, by the overwhelming power of the heterosexual world. At the same time, it hints at the opposite threat (or promise): that the gay river might overflow its banks, that the old, homophobic story about queers who corrupt "the innocent" might be coming true.

Both positions are true. Gay men and lesbians are real; their sexual desires, like those of heterosexuals, are often quite predictable; and they have common interests and a need, ability, and right to organize politically around those interests. At the same time, their personal identities are not necessarily static, any more so than are the identities of heterosexuals. Their communities are historically shaped and will change in the future.

Biologically determinist theories of sexual orientation are in tune with the mood of an era awash in disappointment. We are confronted with the depressing recognition that an earlier age's hopes of social progress have been frustrated or stalled. Increasingly we must reckon with the dangerous consequences of our technologically centered culture's quest to dominate and exploit the biosphere. Nature, it appears, may have the last word after all—so is it not perfectly reasonable to conclude that biology really is destiny? Certainly the AIDS epidemic offers cruel proof of the power that biological forces potentially wield over individual bodies and social arrangements.

Biological theories have a hopeful side, holding out the promise of strengthening gay identity and community by ratifying the reality of same-sex desire. But they pose their own dangers as well: the danger of reducing an entire universe of diverse same-sex desires and behaviors to fit within an explanatory model based on the experiences of a narrow sample of white, affluent gay North American men; the danger that many people (especially lesbians, bisexuals, and same-sex lovers with roots in other sexual systems) will be excluded because their desires appear to be confused, perverse, imagined, or deficient; the danger of abandoning all the radical potential of outsider identities in favor of consolidating a gay minority status modeled on borrowings from patriarchal culture; the danger that a two-tier system of gayness will be created, in which some people (those with "the gene," for example) are considered "really gay" and others are still "potential heterosexuals" (remember Havelock Ellis and his true invert theory?); and perhaps worst of all, the danger of forgetting that the products of culture—the identities we have made, our socially constructed desires—are every bit as real, significant, and precious as hypothalamic nuclei or bits of DNA.

7

⊞

"That Old Grating Mysterious Engine"

Even in this scientifically oriented society, artists ultimately may have as much to tell us about the mystery of desire as do scientists. This drawing is by the early 20th-century Viennese artist Egon Schiele.

THIS BOOK BEGAN WITH three questions:

1. Is sexual orientation an inborn trait, or does it somehow develop in the unfolding personality?

2. Is it an unchanging characteristic, or one that's liable to shift over time?

3. Is it present in all cultures, even those that appear to organize sexuality quite differently from the way we do, or is it simply the way in which certain societies (especially Western, urbanized ones) currently think about personal sexual identity?

These questions represent the terms of an ongoing debate that my book obviously could not hope to settle but that I have tried to represent fairly. At the same time, I've presented a point of view that may have allowed you to guess something of my own position, which I will now summarize.

Of reputable scientific researchers working today,

none has presented (or even claims to have presented) convincing evidence that anyone's sexual orientation is entirely determined by biological factors; all speak of interactions between inborn characteristics and environment. Yet some do lean toward determinism in that they grant biology a very significant role in explaining what orientation is and how it comes about. I reject this determinism, without dismissing the possibility that we will someday understand a lot more about how inheritance and other factors combine to encourage particular sets of complex behaviors.

Any such understanding will have to transcend monocausal explanations. Biological research in isolation is not a fruitful way to go about comprehending sexuality. Researchers need to pay far more attention to the psychology, sociology, and anthropology of gay, lesbian, bisexual, and heterosexual identities—not, as in the past, based on the notion that all same-sex or opposite-sex desire is a single phenomenon of which a unified account can be given, but with much more sensitivity to the diversity of sexuality.

People's orientations can and do change, which is not to say that everyone's can change, that people make changes at will, or that there is any positive value to be attached either to changing or not changing. I do not believe that the fact that sexual desire can be unpredictable or contradictory means that we are doomed to live in chaos, but neither are we privileged to enjoy infinite possibility. In the poetic formulation of Chicana lesbian writer Gloria Anzaldúa, "Identity is a river."

I am not swayed by the argument that admitting the possibility of flexibility in some people's sexual orientation might give ammunition to bigots. Bigots are not motivated by logic and can find ammunition anywhere; most of them would not be moved to tolerance by evidence that sexuality is biologically determined, and they are in fact all too likely to interpret innate difference as innate inferiority.

As for the third question, most cultures have not shared the modern Euroamerican notion that people are divided into distinct types based on the gender of their preferred sexual partners. More and more is being learned about the fact that what we call "sexuality" is a modern Western concept; the assumption that it is a universal term must be suspended in order to understand sexual behaviors and meanings in other times and places. At the same time, gender—however it may be defined and experienced in a particular culture—appears to be an omnipresent element in the language of desire. Thus it makes sense that people in widely varying cultures would develop sexual tastes based on specifically gendered ways of desiring. The notion of orientation is a subset of possible gendered modes of desire, based on aspects of the Euroamerican gender system.

I recognize that this framework does very little to explain why, given particular sets of culturally defined options, individuals develop as they do. Although such explanations might not be demanded in a less homophobic world, that does not mean the question is intrinsically

The play and movie Grease *illustrate ways in which popular culture transmits images about gender and desire. In the film version, Sandy (played by Olivia Newton-John) is initially too straitlaced to hold the sexual attention of Danny (played by John Travolta), the object of her affections.*

homophobic. Curiosity is likely to be strongest in situations where another outcome seems much more logical—when, for instance, someone grows up lesbian or gay in a conservative community where there are no open homosexuals; or when seemingly identical circumstances produce opposite results. As a man who is an identical twin told researchers Bailey and Pillard, "Sexual orientation is such an important part of my life—anyone's life—that I'm . . . curious why I turned out gay and my brother straight."

Is there nothing more to be said about "that old grating mysterious engine," as writer Dorothy Allison calls sexual desire? Poets, novelists, and visual artists have probably gotten further than theorists in their explorations of the experience of desire—who we are, how we feel when under its spell. But where does it come from? If it is "socially constructed" in some important sense, how does that construction happen at the individual level? How can anything that originates in structures outside of us possess such power and urgency? How does it come to participate in the very core of the self?

At this point, I would like to offer a couple of examples from my own observations and experiences that I think can help illuminate these questions. These instances are quite personal to me; they reflect my gender and my cultural background in ways that may or may not strike a chord with you. But that, after all, is part of the point: if notions of social construction have any value, they suggest that there is no "desire in general," only particular forms of it. The hope is that my own ideas will encourage you to develop your own.

The first example is intended to suggest something about the ways in which young children come to participate in culturally available sexual meanings. On a recent occasion, I spent time with three young daughters of friends, ages seven to ten, and observed their fascinated reactions to the movie *Grease*, which with almost diabolical skill communicates traditional gender messages while drawing the viewer into a hypnotic world of heterosexual myth.

The climax of the story involves the heroine's attempt to realize her destiny and achieve happiness by securing the attentions of a man. The film lavishly illustrates what heterosexual desire is supposed to be, in scenes with mating rituals of dancing and flirting. What struck me was that the little girls seemed to focus—as indeed, the presentation encouraged them to do—not on the rather bland attraction of the male star but instead on the seductive beauty of the woman. I watched them identify with the eroticized thrill of being that woman, desired on screen but desirable, also, to the viewer.

After the movie, one of the girls began to talk about the story, commenting to her mother in reverential tones on her favorite part. What interested her was the point when Sandy, the heroine, decides that she has to stop being such a mousy, good-girl type and instead adopt a more blatantly seductive sexual style if she wants to get her guy. Sandy changes her hairdo, but that is not all. "She seemed prettier. And kind of sweeter, too," Libby shyly reported.

An obvious interpretation is that Libby was learning how to be a feminine sex object. I thought this was part of it but believed I saw a more complicated process at work. It seemed to me that she was also learning both how to desire the condition of being desired and how to desire a woman. The camera's-eye view gave her an opportunity to adopt several different positions—to put herself in Sandy's place but also to see from the outside the effects of the makeover. And in seeing all this, Libby was not just learning about the erotic, but participating in it on a powerful fantasy level.

In this sort of transaction, I believe I can glimpse the origins of the bisexual potential that Weinberg and his colleagues talk about; I also see it as an example of Michel Foucault's idea that sexual desire is not just culturally shaped but produced. The very fact that women are so often visually objectified in our society gives everyone, including little girls, plentiful opportunities to take up the position of spectator, the one for whom feminine beauty is displayed. Of course that is supposedly the male viewpoint. But what guarantee is there that only males will react in this fashion? And how can one separate learning that it is desirable to be or look a certain way from learning to desire those qualities in another?

When I had recently come to identify myself as a lesbian, I reinterpreted what I remembered of my childhood interest in feminine

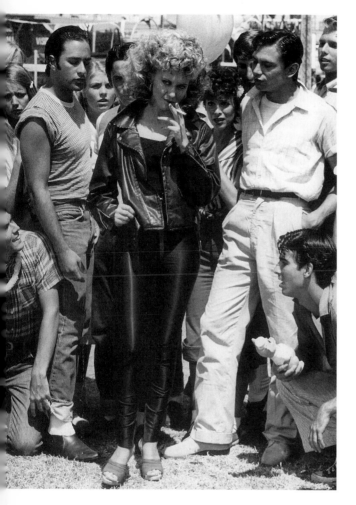

In the film Grease, *it is only after Sandy undergoes a transformation of appearance and behavior, making use of gestures and dress that are understood as advertising her sexual availability, that she is able to "get her man."*

appearance. When I used to cut out glamorous pictures from women's magazines—so I reasoned—it had been because I found those women attractive, not because I wanted to resemble them. I now see that both interpretations were probably valid. I suspect there are parallels in male experience; just think, for instance, of how the visual media glorify and objectify the bodies of male athletes.

My second example is by way of analogy to an impulse that, like sexual desire, is closely connected to notions of "proper" womanhood.

The urge to mother, like the urge to mate, has often been explained as instinct—think of all the references to a woman's biological clock—but I believe its roots are predominantly social and cultural. Not mothering or not desiring to mother exposes a woman to suspicions of being somehow deficient, in a way that echoes and reinforces the stigma of "deviant" sexuality. Like most women who are not biological mothers, I have had to think quite a lot about these issues. (The fact that I have raised a nonbiological daughter, important as it is to me, is not seen as the same thing as bearing a child and does not seem to let me off the cultural hook.) Over the years in which I have watched a number of my woman friends—lesbian and straight alike—become consumed with the passion to parent, I have puzzled over what it is I "lack." The yearning seems to resemble sexual desire in its strength and persistence; those under its spell often seem to feel that life will be incomplete, and they will be less themselves, unless it is fulfilled.

It is easy to see that our society rewards motherhood on a variety of psychic and symbolic levels, despite the ways that the actual work of mothering is so often devalued and unsupported. What is mysterious is not how social incentives work but rather how the image of the relationship between woman and child gets inserted into the very core of the self—becomes part of its skeleton structure. That process seems to me integral, as well, to understanding desire, for at the moment when we desire, we cannot imagine "I" (whoever "I" is) existing without the desire, or with some other set of desires.

I do not have the mother-lust and so do not fully comprehend it in my friends. I suppose I must appear to some of them the way asexual people do to me—much harder to understand than those whose desires merely differ from my own. I can speculate at length about the factors in my early life that might have made me prefer the society of adults, caused me to loathe babysitting jobs, and led me to find most small children rather boring instead of the delightful companions many people think they are. I do not believe my feelings were determined so much as shaped in a certain direction by my early relationships and then helped along by subsequent events, like my decision to pursue the financially marginal life of a writer. I do feel that my basic disposition toward mothering has become a deep and relatively unchanging part of my personality; at the same time, I know of other women who have undergone striking transitions from a negative attitude toward having children to a passionate wish to do so.

What I am trying to suggest is that sexual desire is not unique in its status as a deep-seated, intricately rooted, hard-to-explain component of personality. It is merely the mystery we have been most fascinated by—most frustrated in our inability to predict and control. Thinking about how other needs and wants develop might tell us a good deal about our sexual appetites and about how these are organized within cultural frames of reference. The sexual orientations of hetero-, homo-, and bisexuality currently offered by the Euroamerican sexual system are not the only or inevitable ways of organizing sexuality, but for better or worse they are the structures we currently live inside of. Just as I have been forced to take a position on motherhood by virtue of being a woman, so those who live in North America or Europe currently have little choice but to become, as it were, "oriented to the orientations," whether or not we embrace them. I would much prefer to talk about my sexuality as a narrative, a story unfolding in time, rather than as an identity label. But all too often I find myself in situations where nothing less (or more) than a label will do.

My third example concerns the relationship between mental and physical events in my experience of desire. My sexual arousal is predictably affected by the stages of my menstrual cycle. I find that I am more easily excited during the first half of the cycle; about a week before I get my period, it becomes much more difficult to have an orgasm. This periodicity serves as a constant reminder that desire is always anchored in the body. At the same time, I know that my desires have a great deal to do with mental events in the form of fantasies and feelings. Changes in my body influence what happens sexually, but they do not specify or determine what happens. For instance, I can fail to be turned on by direct physical stimulation, but I can also become extremely aroused while sitting in front of my computer and writing about an imaginary sexual scene.

None of this is particularly new or surprising, but I believe it indi-

*"Be patient toward all
that is unresolved in your
heart; try to love the
questions themselves like
locked rooms or books
that are unwritten in a
foreign tongue," advised
the German poet Rainer
Maria Rilke. "The point
is to live everything. Live
the questions now. You
will then gradually, without even noticing it per-
haps, live along some day
into the answer."*

cates how in our everyday lives we can be quite successful at avoiding
the sorts of artificial distinctions between the mind and the body that
tend to haunt theory. I agree with those observers, from philosophers to
biologists, who have pointed out that what is known as Cartesian dual-
ism—the Western habit of treating mind and body as though they were
two different, unattached entities—accounts for a great deal of unfortu-
nate confusion.

We are our bodies. But in a dualist system, to say this almost automatically seems to make us into objects and to wipe out the activity and
influence of thoughts. The trick is not to put Humpty Dumpty together again—to reunite mind and body—so much as it is to find an angle
of vision from which to see that there never was a split. The body can
then be understood as possibility rather than prescription. As historian

Robert Padgug puts it,

> Biological sexuality is only a precondition, a set of potentialities, which is never unmediated by human reality, and which becomes transformed in qualitatively new ways in human society. The rich and ever-varying nature of such concepts and institutions as marriage, kinship, "love," "eroticism," in a variety of physical senses and as a component of fantasy and religious, social, and even economic reality, and the general human ability to extend the range of sexuality far beyond the physical body, all bear witness to this transformation.

The history of attempts to understand sexuality has been plagued with prescriptions masquerading as descriptions. For over 100 years, anxious laypeople have turned to the experts hoping to be enlightened as to the "truth" of their sexual natures, or to be reassured that their desires are acceptable. Explanation becomes validation—or proscription, taboo. The normal becomes what is supposedly according to nature—or perhaps merely a statistical norm, the alleged behavior of large numbers of people.

The emotional charge behind attempts to define and account for sexual orientation stands as a legacy of these hurtful practices, which have excluded so many and disciplined others to stay within the borders of approved behavior. But the wounds will not be healed by advances in knowledge. We already know enough. Instead, we need to work on enlarging the space for different kinds of people to live well with each other. That is a political project, involving large-scale organizing to stop the right-wing forces that are using hateful images of lesbians and gays, as well as of other marginalized groups, to make power for themselves.

Lesbians, gays, and bisexuals have made enormous social progress in the United States in the years since Stonewall, but it has not been enough—not enough to prevent the abandonment of gay communities to fight the AIDS plague in far too much isolation; not enough to forestall the threat that the clock could be turned back. The example of Germany in the early decades of this century provides a frightening precedent. At the beginning of the 1930s, the country hosted an extremely active homosexual liberation movement and a socially open, sexually progressive atmosphere in cities like Berlin. With the rise to power of Adolf Hitler, all sexual tolerance vanished; later, during the war, homosexuals ended up in concentration camps alongside Jews, gypsies, and political leftists. The United States in the 1990s is a very different place, but the parallels in certain right-wing themes are too close for comfort.

Experts can offer many illuminating, if inconclusive, perspectives on sexuality. But just as they cannot end the political crises caused by bigotry and unjust power relations, so they cannot say how desire connects to identity. They cannot tell us what we desire, what our desires mean, which of them are most real or authentic, if or how to act on them, whether they will change in the future, or how best to move from desires and behaviors to descriptions of our selves.

I know a good deal about how painful sexual identity questions can be at times. Writing this book has often been hard precisely because it has forced me to relive memories of the rupture in my sense of self that came when I moved from identifying as exclusively lesbian in orientation to trying to live without a fixed identity. Others will make choices far different from mine—not necessarily having to do with a change in their partners' gender but certainly involved with changing self-understandings.

What we are is not given; it is, rather, to be discovered. Along the path of exploration lies much that we will have to take as it comes, and a surprising amount of room for creative improvisation. We share a hopeful burden—the burden of freedom.

Sources

CHAPTER ONE

My discussion of how the right wing uses attacks on lesbians and gays to further its own agendas has been informed by Sarah Schulman's *My American History: Lesbian and Gay Life During the Reagan-Bush Years* (NY: Routledge, 1994) and Mab Segrest's *Memoir of a Race Traitor* (Boston: South End, 1994). For a sampling of essays by some of the most important contributors to the essentialist-constructionist debate, see *Forms of Desire: Sexual Orientation and the Social Constructionist Controversy,* edited by Edward Stein (NY: Garland, 1990). Carole Vance offers an insightful assessment of both strengths and weaknesses of a social constructionist approach in her essay, "Social Construction Theory: Problems in the History of Sexuality," in Dennis Altman et al., eds., *Homosexuality, Which Homosexuality?: Essays for the International Scientific Conference on Lesbian and Gay Studies* (London: GMP Publishers, 1989). Daniel Halperin's "Is There a History of Sexuality?" appears in Henry Abelove et. al., eds., *The Lesbian and Gay Studies Reader* (NY: Routledge, 1993).

CHAPTER TWO

My discussion of 19th-century women's friendships draws on Carroll Smith-Rosenberg's "The Female World of Love and Ritual," *Signs* 1 (1975) 1-30. Information on Willa Cather comes from Sharon O'Brien's *Willa Cather* (Philadelphia: Chelsea House, 1995). Adrienne Rich's "Compulsory Heterosexuality and Lesbian Existence" is reprinted in *The Lesbian and Gay Studies Reader.* For a positive discussion of the butch-femme tradition, see Joan Nestle, *A Restricted Country* (Ithaca, NY: Firebrand, 1987). Barry Paddock's "Sex Stories" appears in *Domestic Bliss* #1, 1996. Cherríe Moraga's "A Long Line of Vendidas" appears in *Loving in the War Years: Lo que nunca pasó por sus labios* (Boston: South End, 1983). Dorothy Allison's poem, "The Other Side of the Wall," is from her collection *The Women Who Hate Me* (NY: Long Haul Press, 1983). Tomás Almaguer's essay, "Chicano Men: A Cartography of Homosexual Identity and Behavior," is available in *The Lesbian and Gay Studies Reader.*

Material on sexuality in Greece and Rome comes primarily from John Boswell's "Concepts, Experience, and Sexuality" in *Forms of Desire* and from Daniel Halperin's "Is There a History of Sexuality?"; the Robert Padgug excerpt is quoted in Halperin. For practices among the Sambia of New Guinea, see Gilbert H. Herdt, *Guardians of the Flutes: Idioms of Masculinity* (NY: McGraw-Hill, 1981). For the berdache tradition, see Harriet Whitehead, "The Bow and the Burden Strap," in T*he Lesbian and Gay Studies Reader,* and Will Roscoe, "The Zuni Man-Woman" in *OUT/LOOK* 1:2 (Summer 1988) 56-67. Paula Gunn Allen's poem, "Beloved Women," appeared in *Conditions: Seven* (1981) 65-66. Gloria Wekker's "Mati-ism and Black Lesbianism: Two Idealtypical Expressions of Female Homosexuality in Black Communities of the Diaspora" is from *The Journal of Homosexuality,* special issue on the Third World (1993) 145-58. *The Many Faces of Homosexuality: Anthropological Approaches to Homosexual Behavior,* edited by Evelyn Blackwood (NY: Harrington Park Press, 1986), also contributed to my understanding of sexuality in various cultures.

CHAPTER THREE

Hidden from History: Reclaiming the Gay and Lesbian Past, edited by George Chauncey, Jr., Martin Duberman, and Martha Vicinus (NY: NAL Books, 1989), sheds valuable light on historical approaches to understanding the evolution of a modern homosexual identity. The introduction and essays by Leila Rupp and Eric Garber were especially helpful to developing my argument. My account of the emergence of a modern heterosexual identity is based on Jonathan Katz's "The Invention of Heterosexuality" in *Socialist Review* 20:1 (Jan.-March 1990) 7-34. The discussion of the history of sexology and of sexological theories' relationship to notions of "the natural," both here and in subsequent chapters, owes a great debt to Jeffrey Weeks's *Sexuality and Its Discontents: Meanings, Myths, and Modern Sexualities* (London: Routledge, 1985), especially Chapter Four.

I have also drawn on Martin Dannecker's *Theories of Homosexuality,* trans. David Fernbach (London: Gay Men's Press, 1981) and Carroll Smith-Rosenberg's "Discourses of Sexuality and Subjectivity: The New Woman: 1870-1936" in *Hidden from History.* The discussion of Freud relies on Dannecker and on Henry Abelove's "Freud, Male Homosexuality, and the Americans" in *The Lesbian and Gay Studies Reader.* Martin Duberman's *About Time: Exploring the Gay Past* (NY: Gay Presses of New York, 1986) contains vivid first-person testimony on the "tortures of the talking cure." Esther Newton's "The Mythic Mannish Lesbian: Radclyffe Hall and the New Woman" in *Hidden from History* offers a fascinating interpretation of Hall's use of sexological theory.

CHAPTER FOUR

Martin Duberman's *New York Times Magazine* essay on the Matlovich case can be found in *About Time: Exploring the Gay Past.* "The Woman-Identified Woman" by

Radicalesbians is reprinted in *For Lesbians Only: A Separatist Anthology* (London: Onlywomen Press, 1988). *The Lesbian and Gay Studies Reader* includes Adrienne Rich's "Compulsory Heterosexuality and Lesbian Existence." Two of the most influential early anthologies foregrounding the perspectives of lesbians of color are *This Bridge Called My Back: Writings by Radical Women of Color,* edited by Cherríe Moraga and Gloria Anzaldúa (second edition, New York: Kitchen Table Press, 1984), and *Home Girls: A Black Feminist Anthology*, edited by Barbara Smith (New York: Kitchen Table Press, 1983). *In the Life: A Black Gay Anthology* was edited by Joseph Beam (Boston: Alyson, 1986). Interviews on "Queer" by Steve Cosson in *OUT/LOOK* #11 (Winter 1991) 14-23 and "Forum: On the Political Implications of Using the Term 'Queer,' as in 'Queer Politics' 'Queer Studies,' and 'Queer Pedagogy'" in *Radical Teacher* 45 (Winter 1994) 52-57 were my sources for the quotations on "queer" identity.

CHAPTER FIVE

Gisela Kaplan and Leslie Rogers's essay, "Race and Gender Fallacies," in *Challenging Racism and Sexism: Alternatives to Genetic Explanations*, edited by Ethel Tobach and Betty Rosoff (NY: The Feminist Press, 1994), mentions the R. L. Dickinson case and similar instances of homophobic research. William Byne in "The Biological Evidence Challenged" in *Scientific American* (May 1994) 50-55, Dean Hamer in *The Science of Desire: The Search for the Gay Gene and the Biology of Behavior* (NY: Simon and Schuster, 1994), Simon LeVay in *The Sexual Brain* (Cambridge: MIT Press, 1993), and John Money in *Gay, Straight, and In-Between: The Sexology of Erotic Orientation* (NY: Oxford, 1988) provide information on the role of hormones in physiological development and sexual response, as well as on the various theories attempting to link sexual orientation to hormonal influences. William Byne and Kaplan and Rogers note the relationship between early and recent theories that posit the brain as the site of sexual difference. My treatment of sexual dimorphism in rat and human brains draws on LeVay, *The Sexual Brain,* Simon LeVay and Dean Hamer, "Evidence for a Biological Influence in Male Homosexuality" in *Scientific American* (May 1994) 44-49, and Byne's "The Biological Evidence Challenged."

Kathryn Diaz's article, "The Cultural (Mis)appropriation of a Brain Cell Study," in *Gay Community News* (Oct. 6-12, 1991) 9-13 provides a valuable critical perspective on LeVay's research and on the media response. Edward Stein's "Evidence for Queer Genes: An Interview with Richard Pillard," in *GLQ: A Journal of Lesbian and Gay Studies* 1:1 (1993) 93-110, is the source for Pillard's comments on women's sexual orientation, and for Stein's speculation on mental mechanisms. My main sources for Dean Hamer's gene research are LeVay and Hamer's "Evidence for a Biological Influence in Male Homosexuality" and Hamer's *The Science of Desire;* Byne's "The Biological Evidence Challenged" provides a critical perspective. Ruth Hubbard and Elijah Wald's *Exploding the Gene Myth: How Genetic Information Is Produced and Manipulated by Scientists, Physicians, Employers, Insurance Companies, Educators, and Law Enforcers* (Boston: Beacon, 1993), and Anne Fausto-Sterling's *Myths of Gender: Biological Theories about Men and Women* (second ed., NY: Basic Books, 1992), as well as Hamer's book, offer basic insights into genetic research.

CHAPTER SIX

My major sources for the critique of sociobiology and other forms of genetic determinism are Hubbard and Wald's *Exploding the Gene Myth,* Fausto-Sterling's *Myths of Gender,* and Tobach and Rosoff's *Challenging Racism and Sexism,* especially the essays by Val Woodward, Gisela Kaplan and Lesley Rogers, and Garland Allen. The quotation about levels of organization separating gene and behavior is from Kaplan and Rogers. The John Money quote is from his *Gay, Straight, and In-Between.* Gayle Rubin's "The Traffic in Women: Notes on the 'Political Economy' of Sex and Gender" appears in R. R. Reiter, ed., *Toward an Anthropology of Women* (NY: Monthly Review, 1975). Serena Nanda's "Hijras as Neither Man Nor Woman" is in *The Lesbian and Gay Studies Reader.* Quotations and information on the bisexuality study are from Martin S. Weinberg et al., eds., *Dual Attraction: Understanding Bisexuality* (NY: Oxford, 1994). I'm indebted to Jane Hohenberger, Wilber Valenzuela, and Tehea Robie for sharing with me their perspectives on sexual identity.

CHAPTER SEVEN

The quotation by Robert Padgug is from "Sexual Matters: On Conceptualizing Sexuality in History" in *Forms of Desire.*

Further Reading

GAY AND LESBIAN HISTORY AND CULTURE

Abelove, Henry, Michèle Aina Barale, and David M. Halperin, eds. *The Lesbian and Gay Studies Reader*. New York: Routledge, 1993.

Beam, Joseph, ed. *In the Life: A Black Gay Anthology*. Boston: Alyson Publications, 1986.

Duberman, Martin Bauml, Martha Vicinus, and George Chauncey, Jr., eds. *Hidden from History: Reclaiming the Gay and Lesbian Past*. New York: NAL Books, 1989.

Faderman, Lillian. *Surpassing the Love of Men: Romantic Friendship and Love Between Women from the Renaissance to the Present*. New York: Morrow, 1981.

Katz, Jonathan Ned. *Gay American History: A Documentary History*. Rev. ed. New York: Meridian, 1992.

Moraga, Cherríe, and Gloria Anzaldúa, eds. *This Bridge Called My Back: Writings by Radical Women of Color*. 2nd ed. New York: Kitchen Table Press, 1984.

Smith, Barbara. *Home Girls: A Black Feminist Anthology*. New York: Kitchen Table Press, 1983.

SOCIAL CONSTRUCTIONIST PERSPECTIVES

Foucault, Michel. *The History of Sexuality*, *Vol. I*. Translated by Robert Hurley. New York: Pantheon Books, 1978.

Stein, Edward, ed. *Forms of Desire: Sexual Orientation and the Social Constructionist Controversy*. New York: Garland Publishing, 1990.

BIOLOGICAL EXPLANATIONS

Hamer, Dean, and Peter Copeland. *The Science of Desire: The Search for the Gay Gene and the Biology of Behavior*. New York: Simon and Schuster, 1994.

LeVay, Simon. *The Sexual Brain*. Cambridge: MIT Press, 1993.

Money, John. *Gay, Straight, and In-Between: The Sexology of Erotic Orientation*. New York: Oxford University Press, 1988.

CRITIQUES OF GENETIC DETERMINISM

Fausto-Sterling, Anne. *Myths of Gender: Biological Theories about Men and Women*. 2nd ed. New York: Basic Books, 1992.

Hubbard, Ruth, and Elijah Wald. *Exploding the Gene Myth: How Genetic Information Is Produced and Manipulated by Scientists, Physicians, Employers, Insurance Companies, Educators, and Law Enforcers*. Boston: Beacon Press, 1993.

Tobach, Ethel, and Betty Rosoff. *Challenging Racism and Sexism: Alternatives to Genetic Explanations*. New York: The Feminist Press, 1994.

CROSS-CULTURAL PERSPECTIVES

Blackwood, Evelyn, ed. *The Many Faces of Homosexuality: Anthropological Approaches to Homosexual Behavior*. New York: Harrington Park Press, 1986.

Boswell, John. *Christianity, Social Tolerance, and Homosexuality: Gay People in Western Europe from the Beginning of the Christian Era to the Fourteenth Century*. Chicago: University of Chicago Press, 1980.

Herdt, Gilbert H. *Guardians of the Flutes: Idioms of Masculinity*. New ed. Chicago: University of Chicago Press, 1994.

Weeks, Jeffrey. *Sexuality and Its Discontents: Meanings, Myths, and Modern Sexualities*. London: Routledge and Kegan Paul, 1985.

Williams, Walter L. *The Spirit and the Flesh: Sexual Diversity in American Indian Culture*. Boston: Beacon Press, 1986

BISEXUALITY

Clausen, Jan. "My Interesting Condition." *OUT/LOOK* 7 (Winter 1990), 11-21. Reprinted in Richard Holeton, ed., *Encountering Cultures*. Reading, MA: Blair Press, 1995.

Garber, Marjorie. *Vice Versa: Bisexuality and the Eroticism of Everyday Life*. New York: Simon and Schuster, 1995.

Hutchins, Loraine and Lani ka'ahumanu, eds., *Bi Any Other Name: Bisexual People Speak Out*. Boston: Alyson Publications, 1991.

Weinberg, Martin S., Colin J. Williams, and Douglas W. Pryor. *Dual Attraction: Understanding Bisexuality*. New York: Oxford University Press, 1994.

HETEROSEXUALITY

Katz, Jonathan. *The Invention of Heterosexuality*. New York: Dutton, 1995.

Glossary

Determinism The view that complex events can be explained by reference to a single underlying aspect or factor. For instance, in social theory, economic determinism is the view that political and cultural formations are effects of the underlying relationships that produce a society's wealth. Biological determinism is the explanation of human and animal behavior in terms of physiological processes initiated by genes, hormones, and the like.

Essentialism An approach to social phenomena that treats all the members of a group as having in common some universal "essence" independent of historical circumstances. For instance, gender essentialism is the belief that all women, regardless of culture or situation, share some basic attribute(s) above and beyond biological sex. In the sexual orientation debates, essentialism usually refers to the belief that groups that could be meaningfully called gay men, lesbians, or homosexuals have existed throughout history and across the spectrum of world cultures. This differs from the claim, accepted by social constructionists, that people in a vast variety of settings have engaged in same-sex erotic behavior.

Gender A set of cultural interpretations based on the biological differences between male and female anatomy.

Gender identity A person's sense of being female or male. Gender identity does not necessarily correspond to anatomical sex (genitals and internal reproductive organs) or chromosomal sex (XX for females, XY for males—some people are also born with chromosomal variations, such as an extra Y chromosome, XYY, in certain men).

Heterosexism The system that privileges heterosexuals and discriminates against homosexuals; also, complexes of attitudes that reinforce these practices. Heterosexism often operates effectively by making opposite-sex arrangements appear to be universal, natural, and inevitable, thus appearing less offensive than overt homophobic prejudice.

Homophobia The term literally refers to fear of homosexuals, but in practice is used to mean hatred of or prejudice against lesbians, gays, and bisexuals. Unlike "heterosexism," which often refers to institutionalized practices and systems of behavior, "homophobia" more often suggests the conscious or unconscious attitudes held by individuals.

Reductionism An approach that explains the whole in terms of a part thereof. Genetic reductionism is an attempt to understand not just protein synthesis (the specific function determined by genes) but the overall behavior and fate of the organism as an effect of genetic factors.

Sex As distinguished from "gender," the word refers to the biological properties of male and female, i.e. external and internal anatomy and chromosomal makeup. In informal speech, it is often used interchangeably with gender (e.g. "same-sex behavior" instead of "same-gender behavior"). The fact that "sex" also refers to erotic (usually genital) activity indicates the extent to which notions of genital pleasure, gender, and procreation are intertwined in our thinking.

Sexual identity A person's self-identification as a member of a particular social group (e.g. lesbian, heterosexual) based on his or her sexual behaviors or desires. Often used interchangeably with "sexual orientation," although in practice people with different sexual identities may report similar desires and exhibit identical behaviors. For instance, researchers have found that the sexual identity category "bisexual" sometimes overlaps with either "heterosexual" or "homosexual."

Sexual orientation The directedness of a person's desire toward individuals of the same sex (homosexual, gay, lesbian), opposite sex (heterosexual), or both (bisexual). The term "orientation" was adopted to suggest that sexual desire is a relatively stable, unchanging phenomenon, in contrast to "preference" (see below). It is the term commonly though not universally preferred by lesbians and gay men.

Sexual preference Also refers to the directedness of desire, but with the implication that desire is not necessarily fixed.

Sexuality A distinctively modern notion, informed by psychoanalysis and sexology, that tends to equate sexual behavior with the truths of the self. Sexuality is often thought of as a separate realm of experience, like "the economy" or "the state." Individuals are thought to possess a sexuality—a personal sexual "nature."

Social constructionism An approach to social phenomena that seeks to understand human behavior as a product of culture and history rather than of "nature." Social constructionists typically question claims that seemingly similar instances of behavior or group membership in different times and places partake of the same "essential" character and/or are traceable to biological causes.

Sociobiology An attempt to unite aspects of Darwinian evolutionary theory with genetics and the social sciences in order to interpret social phenomena in the light of underlying biological processes.

Transsexual Someone who undergoes a medical procedure to alter anatomical sex to correspond to gender identity. Preoperative transsexuals are people who have begun the process and receive hormone treatments before the final step of surgery.

Index

Jan Clausen has written on literature, feminism, and multiculturalism for such periodicals as *Ms.*, *The Nation*, OUT/LOOK, and *The Women's Review of Books*. A poet and fiction writer, she is the author of the lesbian novels *Sinking, Stealing* (Crossing Press, 1985) and *The Prosperine Papers* (Crossing Press, 1988). She teaches writing and directs the writing center at the Eugene Lang College of the New School for Social Research.

Martin Duberman is Distinguished Professor of History at the Graduate Center for the City University of New York and the founder and director of the Center for Lesbian and Gay Studies. One of the country's foremost historians, he is the author of 17 books and numerous articles and essays. He has won the Bancroft Prize for *Charles Francis Adams* (1960); two Lambda Awards for *Hidden from History: Reclaiming the Gay and Lesbian Past,* an anthology that he coedited; and a special award from the National Academy of Arts and Letters for his overall "contributions to literature." His play *In White America* won the Vernon Rice/Drama Desk Award in 1964. His other works include *James Russell Lowell* (1966), *Black Mountain: An Exploration in Community* (1972), *Paul Robeson* (1989), *Cures: A Gay Man's Odyssey* (1991), *Stonewall* (1993), *Midlife Queer* (1996), and *A Queer World* (1996).